COACHES CLINICS

PRACTICE PLANNING

Edited by
Bob Murrey

D1733604

ISBN: 1-57167-453-5
Library of Congress Catalog Card Number: 99-64113

Cover Design: Jennifer Scott
Cover Photo: Wake Forest University
Series Editor: Deborah M. Bellaire
Production Manager: Michelle A. Summers

Coaches Choice Books is a division of:
    Sagamore Publishing, Inc.
    P.O. Box 647
    Champaign, IL 61824-0647
    http://www.sagamorepub.com

TABLE OF CONTENTS

Chapter 1: Practice Planning 5
Geno Auriemma-Connecticut (Women)

Chapter 2: Conditioning with a Basketball.................................... 21
Jim Foster-Vanderbilt (Women))

Chapter 3: Practice Sessions 39
Pete Gaudet-Duke

Chapter 4: Planning Practice Sessions 47
Seth Greenberg-Long Beach State

Chapter 5: The Little Things That Help 53
Dave Odom-Wake Forest

Chapter 6: Practice Sessions 71
Kevin O'Neill-Marquette

Chapter 7: Sooner Intensity Drills 77
Kelvin Sampson-Oklahoma

Chapter 8: Offensive Alignments... 85
Wimp Sanderson-Arkansas-Little Rock

Chapter 9: Organizational Thoughts 101
Danny Singleton-Atlanta Lovett High School

Chapter 10: Practice Preparation 115
Bob Sundvold-Missouri-Kansas City

Chapter 11: The Daily Practice Schedule 119
Part 1: Defense
Part 2: Offense
John Wooden-UCLA (Retired)

DIAGRAM LEGEND

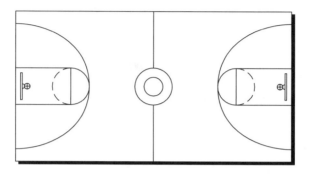

PLAYERS

(5) Centers

(3,4) Forwards

(1,2) Guards

◯ = Offense

X = Defense

◖ = Player with the Ball

— — → = Direct Pass

———⊣ = Screen

⌇⌇⌇→ = Dribble

———→ = Cut of Player Without Ball

⊬⊬⊬⊬⊬→ = Shot

Chapter One

PRACTICE PLANNING

Geno Auriemma

I think that the most important thing you do in coaching basketball is what you do in practice. Whatever you do in practice is going to be reflected in your games. The better you practice, the better you are going to play. I want to keep our players on edge a little. I want them to be intense. I got this at a clinic. You go to clinics to get ideas. Nobody in this room has had an original thought. If you think you have, you're crazy. Don't be afraid to steal ideas and use them. Even against teams in your league. If they do something really good, steal it from them and use it. There is nothing better than beating someone with the things they do. Take whatever you can use from wherever you can get it, and use it.

We have eight baskets, four coaches, twelve players. You probably have two baskets, two coaches and varsity and JV on the floor at the same time. How can you get the maximum use out of the time and the facility that you have? First of all, you must **have a plan.** At the beginning of the season you must have a plan for the whole year. You must treat your team as if you were **teaching a class.** You wouldn't show up in your biology class and just wing it. You must treat your team the same way. You must know what you are going to do in November, December, January, etc. Break it down within each month. What do you want to have in? Break it down each week. What do you want in by the third week? Break it down by the day. You must be prepared every day. Here's the difference. You can be married to that plan and stick with it no matter what (which means you aren't going to be any good) or you can build in some flexibility so that if you need five minutes more you can take it. Don't try to do too many things. This is an idea of what we do every day. We shoot, we work on ballhandling, we work on passing, we play man-to-man defense, and we rebound the ball. We do those things every day in one form or the other. Here is a typical practice for us. We start with a 10-minute individual instruction period.

(Diagram 1) We may have all the guards at one end, and forwards at the other. Each guard has a ball. Each forward has a ball. Today, for example, the guards are going to work on shooting off the dribble. We make the players pass to themselves. Toss the ball out with backspin and go get it. Check their footwork. Shot fake, two-dribble maximum, shoot the bankshot. We aren't going full speed yet. The forwards are passing to themselves and get the ball with the jump stop. Today, they may be working on the drop step. They make the move. If they miss, they must follow it up.

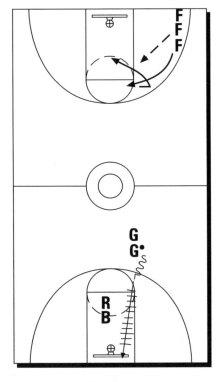

Diagram 1

(Diagram 2) Here's another one. Coach passes to forward after the V-cut is made. Go low, cut high, or go high and cut low. Square up, shoot. If the shot is missed, rebound it and put it back in.

(Diagram 3) Two lines of guards. Come to the manager (the screen), curl around the manager and get the pass from the coach.

(Diagram 4) Guards come off the screen straight out. Square up, and shoot.

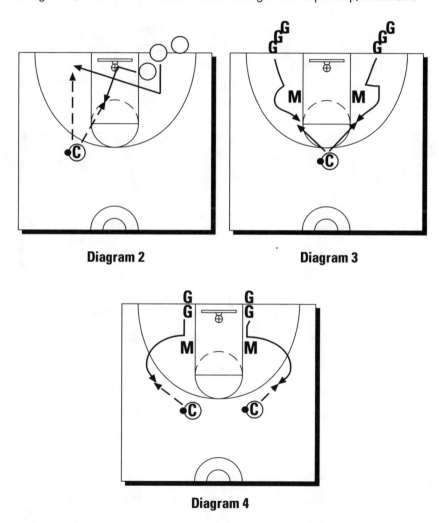

Diagram 2   **Diagram 3**

Diagram 4

(Diagram 5) Use this with the big kids. This is a great drill. Everything Duke does in practice is based on getting shots, shooting the ball. This is one of their drills. Screen down and cut across the lane for the shot. Then, set a backscreen and come back low for a second shot. Break high for the third shot. Someone else rebounds the balls. Don't just stand and shoot. **Move and shoot.** Then, sometimes we stretch. We circle at center court. This is the time when you talk to your players, and if you are mad at them, don't talk to them.

(Diagram 6) We do this drill every day. Two basketballs. Guard takes two dribbles, jump stop. Forward cuts to the basket. Bounce pass, layup. This is a high jump, not a long jump. Put a coach in the drill. The guard goes around the coach in the opposite direction of the pass for the offensive rebound. Why? So we don't charge. We make about 12 in a row.

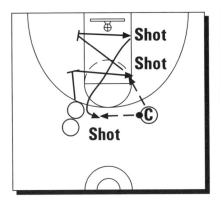

Diagram 5

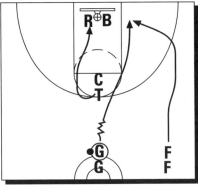

Diagram 6

Diagram 7) Same thing except take the jump shot off the glass. Girls have a hard time stopping and going straight up for the jump shot. We change lines in these drills so that everyone shoots and everyone passes. We make 12 in a row on this drill also.

(Diagram 8) **Four-Corners Passing Drill.** 1 passes to 2. 2 passes back to 1 as 1 is moving toward 2. 1 goes in front of 2 and hands the ball back to 2 and then gets in the end of 2's line. 3 is doing the same thing with 4. You can use up to four balls. Teach your kids to talk. Every time a player passes, she must call out the name of the player receiving the pass.

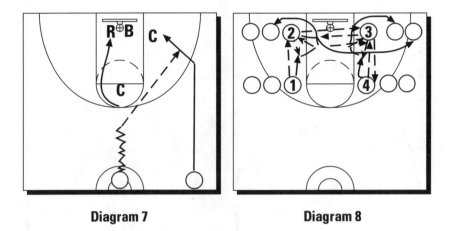

Diagram 7   **Diagram 8**

(Diagram 9) **"Kansas Drill."** I got this from Larry Brown. The big kid under the basket is 4. The other big kids are under the basket out of bounds. Three guards on the floor. Other guards are out of bounds on the sideline. 4 throws the ball off the glass, rebounds, turns and outlets to 1 who goes away and comes back for the pass. 2 goes away and comes back to the center circle. 3 breaks long. The ball goes 4 to 1 to 2. 2 gets one dribble maximum and passes to 3 who catches the ball for the layup. The ball never touches the floor. 4 must grab the ball before it hits the floor at the other end.

(Diagram 10) Coming back, 2 is still in the middle of the floor as 4 rebounds the ball out of the net. 1 and 3 have crossed and are going back. 4 passes to either side, probably to 3 who made the layup. 3 passes to 2 and they go the other way. 2 takes a maximum of one dribble and passes to 1 who catches the ball, stops and shoots a 3-point shot. 4 gets the rebound at the other end.

(Diagram 11) 4 rebounds the 3-point shot, outlets to 1. 2 goes away and comes back for the pass from 1. After the shot, 3 goes long. 2 passes to 3. 3 makes a skip-pass across to 1 who shoots the 3-point shot. 4 rebounds again.

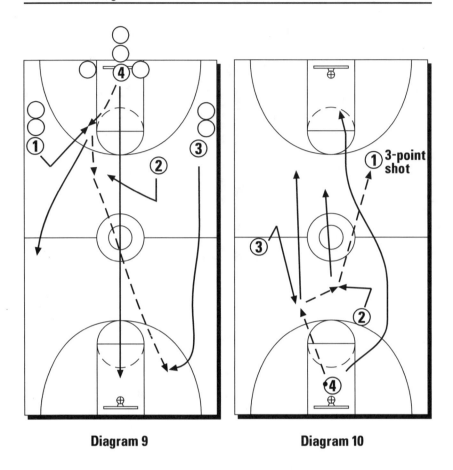

Diagram 9   **Diagram 10**

(Diagram 12) Go back again. 4 to 1 to 2 to 1 to 4 for the layup. The ball can be passed to either wing. This is a great conditioner.

(Diagram 13) Sometimes we change the drill and the big player stops for the 3.

(Diagram 14) **Five-Man Weave.** Pass the ball and go behind two people. We go five-man weave up and the shooter and the passer play defense coming back so it is three-on-two.

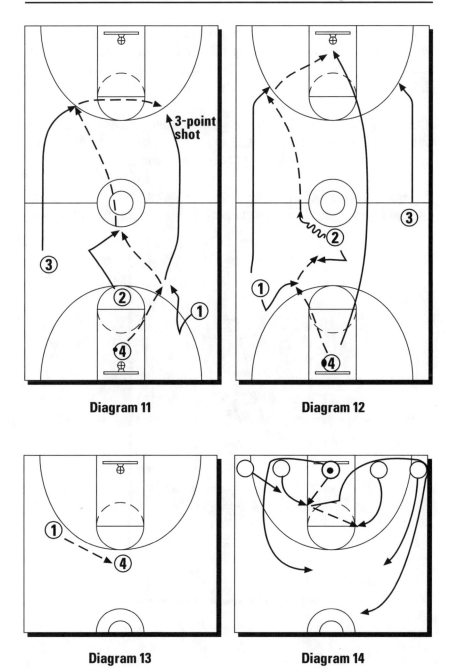

Diagram 11

Diagram 12

Diagram 13

Diagram 14

(Diagram 15) We then do the **11-man break.** Start with three-on-two with 3, 4 and 5 starting this drill against 1 and 2. With either a made shot or with 1 rebounding, 1, 6 and 7 will go the other way against 8 and 9. Either 8 or 9 will come back with 10 and 11.

(Diagram 16) We added this. Suppose 5 shoots and it goes in. Suppose 8 gets the ball and starts back with 9 and 10. The three original offensive players go on defense until the ball gets to half-court.

(Diagram 17) **Shooting drills,** two men at a basket. 30 seconds. Pass the ball for the shot. The passer runs at the shooter, contests the shot

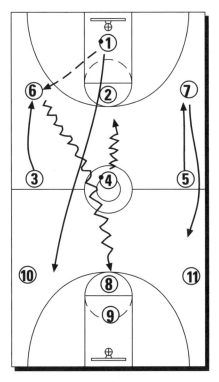

Diagram 15

and then boxes out the shooter. How many shots in the 30 seconds? Then, add a **shot fake.** Then, shot fake and drive.

(Diagram 18) **Two passers, one shooter.** Move from elbow to elbow for the shot. 30 seconds.

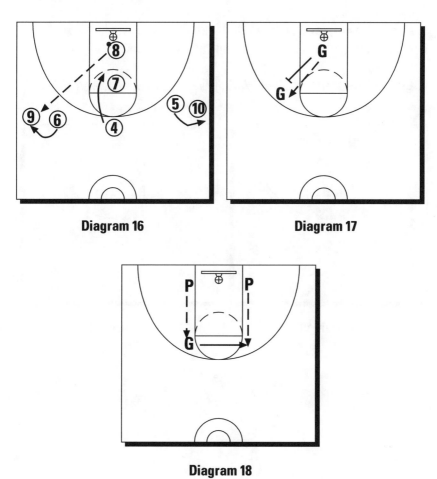

Diagram 16   **Diagram 17**

Diagram 18

(Diagram 19) We use our **big kids** in this area. I don't know why. Part of it is they can't jump. They have a hard time catching the ball with their back to the basket, turning and shooting. Also, we play behind the post all the time. Why? Because girls can't score in the low post. Any shot that you don't make, we expect to get the defensive rebound. And there are no lob passes. We help out with our guards. That's the way we feel. After we do this shooting, in practice we go to individual defense, about a 10-minute segment, and then we go to team defense, another 10-minute segment.

We may do a **help and recover** drill with the guards while we work with denying the flash with the big players. (Diagram 20)

(Diagram 21) We do a lot of **Shell Work,** four on defense and five on offense.

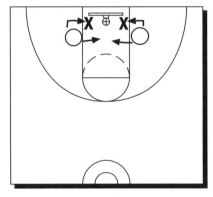

Diagram 19

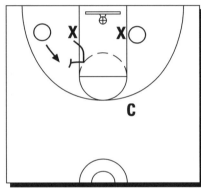

Diagram 20

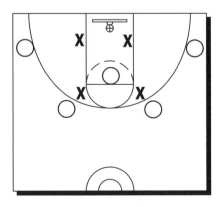

Diagram 21

(Diagram 22) **Six vs. Four.** Every time the player on the baseline gets the ball, she drives to the basket. The opposite forward must come across and stop the ball outside the lane.

(Diagram 23) If we work on the break, we have **random movement** while the coach has the ball. Coach shoots, players block out and then run break five-on-zero. Then, we break for foul shots. For the first time, we shoot ten straight. Get into a rhythm. Anyone who doesn't make at least eight owes a sprint at the end of practice. Then they get a drink of water.

Diagram 22

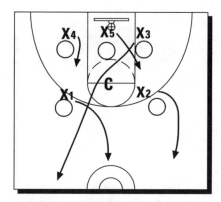

Diagram 23

(Diagram 24) Then, we go to offense. The guards are working using the screen. A guard passes to the coach, screens away. Come off screen, square up, and shoot.

(Diagram 25) A guard passes into the post and relocates. Defense turns to double-team. Don't stand and watch. Move. Our rule is turn opposite the way the defense turns.

(Diagram 26) The post players will be working on the **lateral screen.** Set the screen. If a player goes off the screen low, the screener goes high.

Diagram 24

Diagram 25

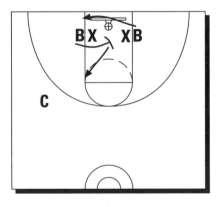

Diagram 26

(Diagram 27) We can do this with a high/low setup.

(Diagram 28) Post players will work on **backscreens.** If the player goes low, the screener comes back for the ball high. Just about everything we do involves shooting drills.

Diagram 27

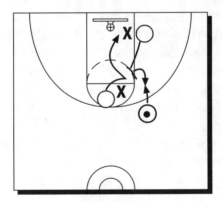

Diagram 28

(Diagram 29) Now we get into **team offense.** Team offense is four-on-four, three teams. Go for ten minutes or the first team to seven baskets. If the team scores, take the ball to half-court and go again against a different defensive team. The only way you get on offense is to rebound a missed shot or force a turnover. **Make the teams competitive.** We don't scrimmage a lot. We control our scrimmages. If the defense gets a turnover, they run the break. They must score on the break. If they don't because of a miss or a turnover, we stop the play. We run half-court offense. If the defense gets the ball, they run the break to the other end.

(Diagram 30) Then, we work on the **press offense.** 4 is a big player. 1 is the point guard, 5 is the other big player. We start with a 1-4. The ball goes into 3, 1 goes to the middle, 4 is the trailer, 2 goes long. You must have the same thing for every press.

(Diagram 31) Early in the year we work on shooting the **foul shot.** When we are working on press offense, we let the other team shoot and attack the press. We end practice with some type of quickness drill, maybe a full-court passing drill or a zigzag drill. Then we will do ten minutes of individual work with several players. This is about two and one-half hours. We never practice more than that. From January on, we practice for about an hour. We take some days off, especially after a night game on the road. We don't practice longer if we lose a game. Don't let the team that beat you on Wednesday night beat you Saturday. Forget about Wednesday and get on with the next game. Sometimes we will stop practice and talk to the team for five minutes.

I'll guarantee you that when they start practice again they will be terrible. Why? They lost their concentration. But that's the same as halftime, right? So, teach them in practice to stop play, listen, and go out with the same concentration and enthusiasm.

Diagram 29

Diagram 30

Diagram 31

Chapter Two

CONDITIONING WITH A BASKETBALL

Jim Foster

How many people here run suicides or sprints in practice? I'm going to give you a series of drills that may change your mind. I think that you are coaching basketball because you like to coach basketball, and if you really wanted to coach track, you would. I think that any time you can get your players to run with a basketball, you are doing your kids a service and you are not wasting time. Time has become a very important factor with us. We have twenty hours a week that we can practice. This may seem like a lot, but in reality it's not when you have conditioning, weight training, video sessions, etc. That all has to fit in the twenty hours. So, running for running's sake wastes time. We have not run a suicide for the last fourteen years. We will run sprints, just up and back, to differentiate between winning and losing in competition. Most of the things we do are competitive. Most of the things we do are against the clock and can be done with a very good manager. We don't take a layup in practice that isn't counted.

We start our practice with what we call **"three tight."** This is the full-court weave, pass and go behind, and the players are as tight as they can get. When they get to the other end of the floor they must make the layup. If they don't, the group of three does five pushups. This gets their concentration level to where it should be. If your players can't do pushups, they do situps. You must make layups. We don't start practice until the whole team goes up and back. Then, we go **"three wide."** This is the same drill except the players are wider. Go up and back. It is the same principle. They must make the layup. Everyone must make a layup so we switch lines and go up and back three times.

(Diagram 1) This is our **"pitch and fill"** drill. We always run this on the left side of the floor and we always take a left-handed layup. 1 throws the ball against the glass and rebounds. 1 then pivots and makes an outlet pass to 4. 4 dribbles to the foul line extended. 1 runs wide and cuts at a 45-degree angle to the basket and gets a bounce pass from 4. 1 must make a left-handed layup. Don't make it? Do situps or pushups. Switch lines. We use three balls, two at one end, one ball at the other. We do this for two minutes. We always run this on the left side of the floor.

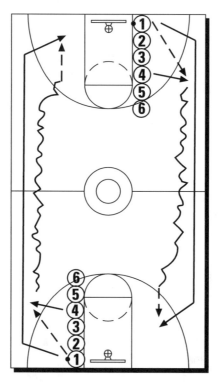

Diagram 1

(Diagram 2) Now we do **"handle."** This is a very simple, fundamental drill. We have two coaches on the floor. Use half as many balls as you have players. 1 starts on the dribble. We have a rule that you are not allowed to use the crossover dribble in front of a guard. We assume that the first coach is a guard. When 1 gets to the first coach, 1 must make a behind-the-back move, through the legs, or the spin. At the next coach, you assume that the coach is not a guard so you may use any type of move. 1 stops near the foul line for the jump shot. This drill is done for three minutes. For the first minute and a half the ball is in the right hand so that the dribble move is made from the right to the left. For the next one and one half minutes the ball is in the left hand and the dribble move is made from their left to their right. After the jump shot, get your own rebound and speed dribble back with the left hand. Just over half-court they make a sharp, crisp pass to the next person in line. We have just started practice and we have worked on passing, lefthanded layups, stopping at the foul line, and ballhandling. Every player on the team does this. I think sometimes we stereotype our big players; i.e., we don't let them dribble. We make all our players do these drills. Your centers should be able to handle the ball.

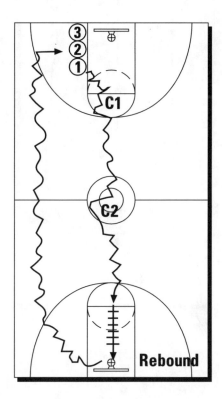

Diagram 2

(Diagram 3) **Full-court Shooting Drill.** 7 and 8, 4 and 6 each has a ball, as does 1. 1, 2, and 3 will start this continuous drill. We run this drill for three minutes and set a goal of 100 points. You get one point for a jump shot, and two points if you make a three. 1, 2, and 3 start down the floor passing back and forth. 1 to 2 to 1 to 3 to 1. By this time 1 is near the foul line. 1 takes a jump shot from the foul line area. 2 gets a pass from 7 and 3 gets a pass from 8. 2 and 3 each shoot. 1 gets the rebound and starts the other way with 7 and 8. 2 and 3 rebound their shots and stay at the end taking the place of 7 and 8.

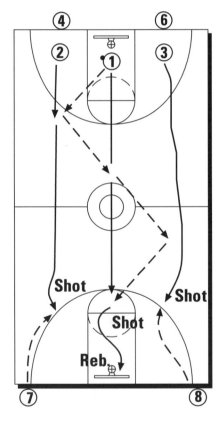

Diagram 3

(Diagram 4) 4 and 6 are waiting with balls to feed 7 and 8. 1 gets another jump shot at the foul line. Count every ball that goes in the basket. 1 then goes to the end of the line behind 5 and 5 goes the next trip. Remember, one point for a traditional field goal, two points for a 3. We have now been on the floor for two minutes for **"tight"** and **"wide,"** two minutes for **"pitch and fill,"** three minutes with **"handle,"** and three minutes with **"fullcourt shooting."** You, as a coach, must pick a realistic total to make in three minutes.

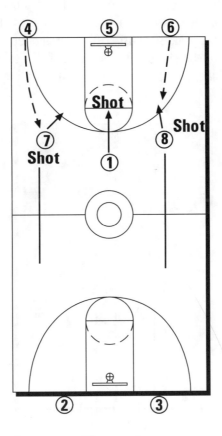

Diagram 4

(Diagram 5) **Four Pass Drill.** We use three balls. 1, 2, and 3 have balls. 1 makes an overhead outlet pass to 4. After throwing that pass, 1 sprints full-court. 4 pivots toward the sideline and throws a baseball pass to 7. 7 catches the ball, pivots, and makes a bounce pass to 1 for the layup. 1 scores and flies the other way. 7 rebounds. 7 throws a lead, two-hand chest pass over the head of 1.

We teach our players to put **reverse English** on the ball so that when the ball hits the floor it bounces up. If needed, 7 is allowed to take one dribble. 1 must track down the pass. We like the pass to land just over the center circle. 7 is going to chase after 1. 1 will dribble for the layup and 7 must catch the ball before it hits the floor, pivots and throws the ball to the outlet line. This is a continuous drill and all three balls should be going at once.

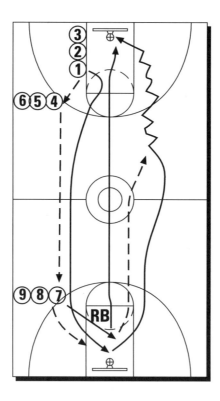

Diagram 5

(Diagram 6) 1 goes to the baseball pass line, 4 to the bounce pass line, and 7 to the outlet pass line. During the course of this drill we keep makes and misses on the scoreboard. The home team gets the makes, the visiting team gets the misses. We chart everything. For our team, we have gone 72 and 0. If we miss 3 or 4, we do it again. This is relative to the level at which you are coaching, but you must make them accountable. You must keep their interest and they like the fact that it is competitive. You can let 7 put back a missed layup if 7 gets to the ball before it hits the floor. That's up to you. We run this for three minutes.

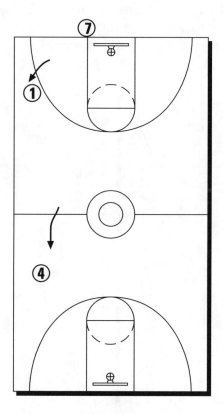

Diagram 6

(Diagram 7) **"Six Spots."** 1 through 6 don't move. 1 faces 6, 3 faces 4. 2 and 5 have their backs to each other. 6 through 12 each has a ball. 7's and 10's first pass is a two-handed chest pass to 2 and 5. 7 and10 start up the floor and get the ball back from the person they threw the pass to. As 7 is throwing to 2, 8 is throwing the ball to 1, and 11 is passing to 4. When 7 gets the ball back from 2, the pass is made from 7 to 3. 7 gets a return bounce pass from 3 and takes the layup. The same thing happens in the other direction.

(Diagram 8) 9 passes to 1, and 12 passes to 4 and six players are moving. All passes are chest passes except the bounce pass for the layup. The players get their own rebounds and start again. 7 passes to 1, but if it is congested, 7 can pass directly to 2. The same for 10.

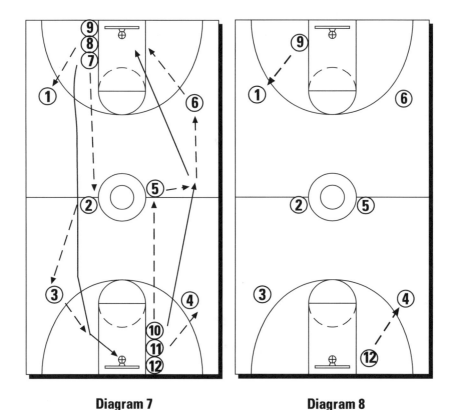

Diagram 7   **Diagram 8**

This is a continuous drill. Count makes and misses. Some players should get eight trips up the floor. If we go 46 and 0, I'm happy. A 42 and three makes me unhappy. I don't think my team should miss three layups, but it is relative to the level. Go every other day right-handed side, every other day left. If you get bunched up, skip the short pass and make the pass to half-court. You switch so that the six people on the floor will get their turn to run. We run this for a minute. This was my first year with this team. And when we started they were dying. They had never been held accountable. They just ran drills to run drills. And now I'm there saying , "do it again, that's not good enough." By the end of the year this was by far the best drill team I ever had. In the **"4 pass drill"** I wanted at least 70 makes. In this drill I wanted a minimum of seven trips, or 42 attempts (with six people running). This told me where they were mentally. And we practiced at 6:00 in the morning! I think you can condition, teach, and also get them to concentrate.

(Diagram 9) The last drill for cardiovascular purposes is called **"Celtic,"** an old Celtic drill. Use three balls, time for four minutes, count makes and misses. 1 makes an outlet pass to 6. 6 pivots toward the sideline, and dribbles down the floor for the layup. 1 sprints down the floor to the foul line, goes wide and starts back. 6 gets her own rebound and throws a baseball pass to 1. 1 dribbles for the layup. We want 6 to get the ball out of the net, before it hits the floor. Again, make it relative to whom you are coaching. 6 and 1 will switch lines. Three balls continuously. As soon as 1 and 6 get to about half-court, 2 and 7 start, etc. Do this for four minutes. The best we got was 115 and 0, in four minutes. This is the only drill we don't flip sides on. We just haven't. We just go right-handed to go after the high numbers.

(Diagram 10) We do the **"Full-court Tap Drill"** for the next minute. Tap the ball off the glass, run down the floor where a coach throws another ball off the glass. They go back and forth. Then we go to the foul line. We have not run a suicide or a sprint, but we have conditioned for over one-half hour.

(Diagram 11) **Eleven-Man Continuity.** Start with 1, 2, and 3 going against 4 and 5. 6 and 7 are outlets, as are 8 and 9. 10 and 11 are

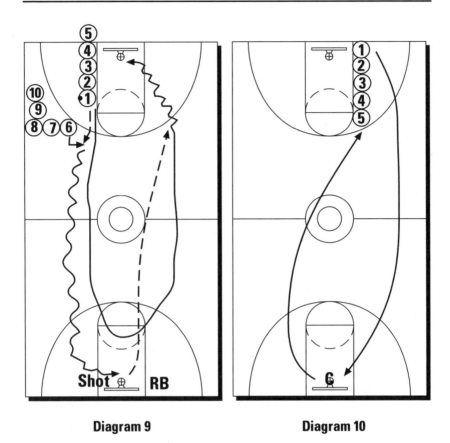

Diagram 9   **Diagram 10**

defenders at the other end. Play 3-on-2, and after a turnover or a made shot, whoever gets the rebound or takes the ball out of bounds will make an outlet pass to either 6 or 7. Suppose that 5 gets the rebound and outlets to 6. 6 goes middle. 7 and 5 fill the lanes and now they are going against 10 and 11. 4 will rotate into the outlet line as will 1. 2 and 3 will assume the defensive positions at this end of the floor.

(Diagram 12) Now it looks like this. We run this for five minutes. You get a point if you score from inside the three-point line, you get two points for a three. I think that 3-on-2 is a good time to shoot the three. If you shoot 33% from three-point range, it is the same as shooting 50% from two-point range. I am partial to the three-point shot. Our two best three-point shooters this year had never taken a three in their life before this

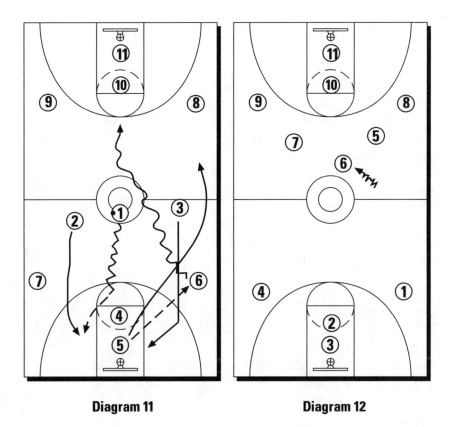

Diagram 11   **Diagram 12**

year. One of them shot 54% in the SEC for threes. We want the team to get 25 points in five minutes.

(Diagram 13) **4 on 3, 3 on 4.** Our colors are black and gold, so we have a black team and a gold team. Coach is near the foul line. Three gold players with the coach, four blacks against gold. The black guarding the coach is passive. The only one who can shoot from the perimeter is the coach, who tries to miss. The gold players pass and cut. The coach either shoots or just passes to the black team, simulating a turnover.

When this happens the black team runs the break. The outside lanes are filled and one player goes to the block. The point guard has the ball. The gold team drops back on defense. When this happens you will get a shot unless you are careless with the ball. I know you work 2-on-1 drills, and 3-on-2 drills. How many times do you work 4-on-3? We should because it happens many times in a game.

(Diagram 14) After the score, we now have the 3-on-4 part. If you miss, it is still 3-on-4. If you are getting ready to play against a 1-2-1-1 press, align the black team in a 1-2-1. Change to whatever you need, faceguard, run and jump, trap, etc. Change people so that there are now four gold and three black. You can work on anything that you want.

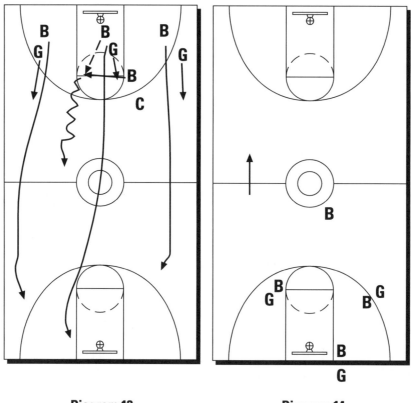

Diagram 13   **Diagram 14**

(Diagram 15) Suppose you are going to work on 3's today. You come down the floor, 1 is the point guard, and 4 is the trailer. Someone is going to get a 3-point shot; three people can't guard four people.

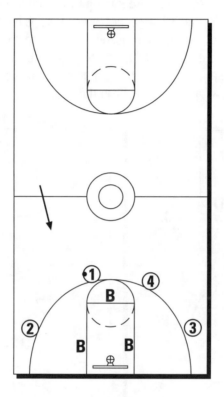

Diagram 15

(Diagram 16) Here is a drill for **shooting 3's.** This has some of the rules of the old girls' game. You are not allowed to cross half-court. It starts with a jump ball. Letters go against numbers. We play this for ten minutes. 5 and A will jump. Once it is tapped, it is the last time that 5 and A will be on those ends of the floor. Now it's 3-on-2. It is a continuous attempt to shoot 3's. Let's say that 5 gets the tip. Now you have 5, 2, and 3 against D and E. They are going to do whatever they need to do to shoot a 3 (Diagram 17). It can be dribble penetration, skip-passes, whatever. The only baskets you are allowed to score are a 3, an uncontested layup, or an offensive rebound for a layup. We need to be able to score the layup to keep the defense from cheating. For example, 5 could dribble penetrate, pass out to 3 who makes the skip-pass to 2 for the shot. We like to make **"the next pass"** whenever possible, the next shorter pass for the 3. I like penetration or skips before shooting the 3. We are going to constantly be successful because it is 3-on-2. You get two points for a three, one for a layup. This drill is ten minutes in length and they compete against each other for score. On a good day the score will be in the 30s, a bad day it will be in the 20s.

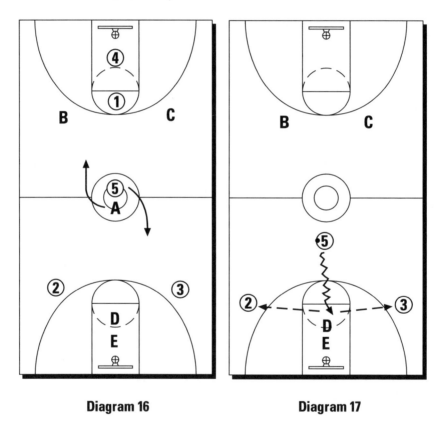

Diagram 16   **Diagram 17**

(Diagram 18) Suppose they score. It is now 2-on-3. E inbounds to D. 5 is on the inbounder, 2 and 3 doubleteam D. The first pass must be made in the back-court. After the ball gets inbounds, the pass may be made across halfcourt and A, B, and C attack 1 and 4. But don't keep the defenders back in the lane. They can be anywhere, but they can't go across half-court. Anytime that the ball is deflected and knocked out of bounds, the ball is brought back and inbounded from the end line again, 2 vs. 3.

(Diagram 19) We made an adjustment for our big kid (5). One of the two defensive people had to guard her so that left one of the two defenders to guard two perimeter players. We would feed the post, trap, and look for the pass back out for the three-point shot.

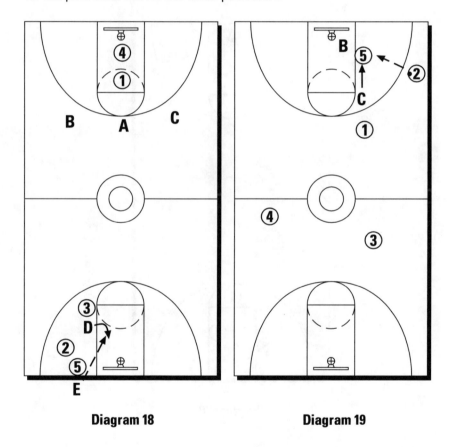

Diagram 18   **Diagram 19**

(Diagram 20) **Recognition Drill.** One coach is along the sideline with a number of players. There are five players on the court with another coach. Coach will either make a layup, miss a shot, or simulate a turnover by throwing the ball to one of the players. Whatever the coach does, the drill starts out 5/0. The other coach has assigned either 1, 2, 3 or more for defense that particular time down the floor. So, the offense must read the defensive numbers. The coach may also send several out on defense and have another wait and trail the play as a defender or challenge the player with the ball coming down the floor. You may get 5-on-3, or 5-on-4. They may be in a zone. They may trap. We go down once, and come back.

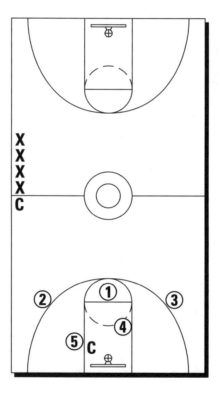

Diagram 20

(Diagram 21) Here's how we come back. We have another coach in the corner with a ball. Let's say that we had 5-on-3 and we scored. The coach in the corner passes to another coach at half-court. The five players who just scored must sprint back to get into whatever defense you want, and stop this coach with the ball. We played a lot of matchup this year, so we ran back to spots. It's called getting back on defense.

(Diagram 22) When we worked against teams who liked to shoot threes we did this same drill but had two extra players on the floor to shoot the threes. The coach would either throw the ball ahead to them or dribble and the emphasis then was for our wings to get back and guard those wings. If the team likes to penetrate, we will be much tighter.

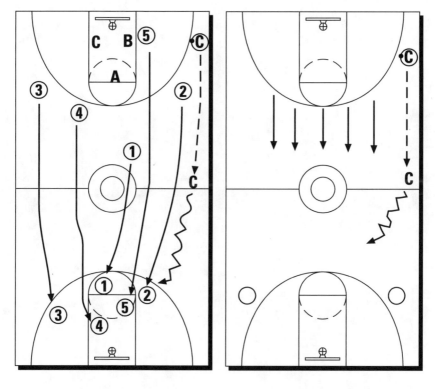

Diagram 21   **Diagram 22**

Chapter Three

PRACTICE SESSIONS

Pete Gaudet

In order to properly develop team play, individual skills and game-like execution in practice, **a work ethic becomes the most essential aspect for success.** Coaches often desire to get their players to play hard all of the time, and a team's practice structure and practice intensity will often dictate their level of intensity in competition. Therefore, the practice atmosphere is the beginning of the players' attitudes and habits concerning hard work and work ethic. As coaches, we often negate our intention to run practices that promote hard play by spending entirely too much time on lecturing. Therefore, it is recommended that practices flow with minimal lecture time. And, above all, practices should be conducted with game-like, live competition in order to prepare players to play hard on a daily basis.

At Duke, terms are employed to promote practice intensity. First, **keep everyone busy by utilizing managers** to free up coaches to coach. Second, keep everyone talking as **communication is essential** in order to allow players to play and execute at full speed. Oftentimes coaches can minimize instructional commands during practice, thus creating a communication deficit that players will fill. This tactic is an excellent method of assessing leadership, as well as the players' degree of comprehension of the system. Third, employ as much live, **game-like competition** as possible. It is recommended that, late in the season, this tactic be curtailed to a certain extent to prevent the occurrence or reoccurrence of injury.

A fourth phase, **yearly practice plan,** is recommended for proper organization and emphasis of specific points at particular times. Practice schedules, written daily, are a must in order to address all points necessary. Practice activities should differ slightly depending upon the time of the year.

The practice year begins with **phase one, pre-season practices.** These are generally the longest practices of the year, lasting an average of two and one-half hours. Individual skill work accompanies drills and scrimmaging that emphasize teaching, establishing habits, installing offensive and defensive systems and experimenting with player combinations. This phase is a time for experimentation with streamlining a program's offensive and defensive systems.

During **phase two, or in-season practices,** emphasis should be placed on improvement on a daily basis. Identification of offensive or defensive strategies that are not effective is highly recommended at this time. It is only logical to dwell on the points that yield success and to abolish the items that your players either cannot understand or cannot execute. Individual work on points of weakness is highly recommended on a daily basis. Improvement of skills is most successful in producing a sound work ethic if emphasized daily.

Phase three generally falls into the period of **conference play.** Practices should be shortened to avoid burn-out and limited contact will reduce the chance of injury. Emphasis at this time should be placed on the team's mental preparation to play, as maintaining intensity levels and focus are crucial to success. A coach must be aware of any type of slippage that may occur, either emotionally or physically. Sloppiness and poor execution should not be tolerated at this point in the season. Finally, in **phase four, or the tournament phase**, a team must be brought within itself emotionally for success to occur. The greatest emphasis in practice should be on execution, rather than searching for methods to combat an opponent's strengths. Know your opponent's tendencies, but prepare yourself to play using the tools that have brought you to this point.

It is our motto at Duke that **defense is an attitude.** Our primary objective in any game is to dominate our opponent defensively in order to achieve success. We intend to make it extremely unpleasant against our pressure defense. Thus, our defensive attitude prepares us psychologically to go out and be physically dominant defensively.

Pressure man-to-man defense must begin with pressure on the ball. The easier it is for a ballhandler to distribute the ball, the less successful the defense. Therefore, any defensive player must be prepared to pressure the ball when his assignment is in possession of it. In order to accomplish this feat, insist that all defensive players maintain a **fundamental defensive stance** until possession is gained. Have confidence in your teammates' abilities to assist you and encourage backdoor cuts and lob passes. In order to achieve this type of pressure, set a number of passes per possession for an opponent and dedicate yourself to making a positive, aggressive defensive play during this period. Finally, and most importantly, insist on **communication and defensive execution** for ultimate success.

Three typical practice schedules are shown—early season, mid-season, and late season.

Finally, you will find several things included that we use in our program when we want to illustrate a point or motivate a player.

"CHOICE, NOT CHANCE, DETERMINES DESTINY."

"Send the harmony of a great desire vibrating through every fiber of your being. Find a task that will call forth your faith, your courage, your perseverance, and your spirit of sacrifice. Keep your hands and your soul clean, and your conquering current will flow freely."

– Thomas Dreier, American Author

"Nothing can stop the man with the right mental attitude from achieving his goal; nothing on earth can help the man with the wrong mental attitude."

–Thomas Jefferson, Third President

"You all have powers you never dreamed of. You can do things you never thought you could do. There are no limitations in what you can do except the limitations in your own mind as to what you cannot do. Don't think you cannot ... think you can!"

– Darwin P. Kingsley, American Insurance Executive

Perhaps there should be a point in our working life where we feel our contributions have been such that we're entitled to take it easy from that point on.

Maybe there should be, but we doubt there is. The minute we start to relax on our oars, we begin to lose our value. Someone else, with more drive and ambition, could step in and do a better job in our place.

Let's face it—what we accomplished yesterday is water over the dam. More important now is what we can do today and tomorrow. When the things we did yesterday and last year are more important than our ambitions for tomorrow and next year, it's time to let someone else take over.

This may seem like a hard, unfeeling way to look at things—but isn't it the truth? You can't win today's game on last week's press clippings. No success is final—no success can last forever.

People who enjoy success have to plan to keep on succeeding. As each goal is achieved, we must look for a new one and keep on scrambling. That's what keeps life interesting.

When you feel you've "got it made," watch out! It's the first step toward settling back into a pleasant, convenient rut. People who have it "made" are only one step from being has-beens.

Like anyone else who coasts, there's only one place for them to go ... downhill.

Keep alive, keep challenging yourself until the day you quit.

When growth stops, decay begins.

DATE: 29 OCT. '91
DAILY PRACTICE SCHEDULE
PRACTICE #13

TIME	ACTIVITY
3:30 - 3:45	Pre-Practice: Individual Work, Catch and Face, Bobby—3 pters., Box Drill
3:45 - 4:00	STRETCH
4:00 - 4:10	2 Man Drills—include Zig-Zag
4:10 - 4:15	3 Baskets—Catch and Face
4:15 - 4:25	Big Men—Post, Drop-Step, Read the Defense Perimeter Men—Shooting (Pass Fakes), 2 on 0
4:25 - 4:35	2 Baskets—2 on 2 w/ a passer Pick and Roll, Flex Pick
4:35 - 4:45	Motion—5 on 5
4:45 - 4:50	Break—free throws
4:50 - 5:20	Phoenix Series—go 5-on-0 —go 5-on-5
5:20 - 5:25	Break—free throws
5:25 - 5:30	4 Coach Passing—4 Man V—Cut

TIME	ACTIVITY
5:30 - 5:40	Big Men—Flash vs. Zone— Go along baseline Perimeter Men—Box Drill
5:40 - 6:00	Offense vs. 2-3 Zone Break 1-2-2 Zone
7:00	Training Meal
***	Wed.—Full Scrimmage— Uniforms & Warmups

14 JAN. '92
PRACTICE #56

TIME	ACTIVITY
3:00 - 3:30	Pre-Practice: Individual Work—Coach K w/ Grant and Thomas
3:30 - 4:00	Locker Room—NC State Personnel Lounge—Hi-lite Tape
4:00 - 4:15	STRETCH
4:15 - 4:25	4-Corners-Per. Passing, 3-Man Passing Up, F.B.Back, Paired Shooting, No Walks, Post Feed (Man in the Middle)
4:25 - 4:30	2 Baskets—Driving Line— Trace the Ball
4:30 - 4:35	3-on-3 Full-court

TIME	ACTIVITY
4:35 - 4:40	3 Baskets—Catch, Face and Drive
4:40 - 4:50	Bigs—Shooting Per.—Zone Shooting
4:50 - 5:00	5-on-0 Motion
5:00 - 5:05	2 Baskets—Contesting slides—Catch and Go Away
5:05 - 5:10	5-on-5 Def.—4 around 1; Shoot Threes
5:10 - 5:15	Team Shooting

NOTES:
- Place to Eat
- Check officials
- Get your rest

Wed. Schedule: B-Fast—11:00; Shoot—12 to 1; Training Meal 4:45; Ready 8:30

1 APRIL '92
PRACTICE #90

TIME	ACTIVITY
3:15 - 3:45	Pre-Practice: Ind. Work Mike—Tape of Bobby (Univ. Games) Grant, Brian, Thomas—Drive Players' Equipment
3:45 - 4:00	STRETCH

TIME	ACTIVITY
4:00 - 4:10	3-Man Passing up—F.B. Back, Rush Drill, 3-on 3-Recognition
4:10 - 4:15	Perimeter—2 Baskets— Catch, Face and Drive the Middle Post—Shooting
4:15 - 4:35	5-on-5 Motion—vs. #21 (Always double Laettner low) #11—Switch, play off
4:35 - 4:45	5-on-5 to 44 - 21, to 34 -14
4:45 - 4:50	Break—Free throws
4:50 - 5:00	2 Baskets—Contesting Slides Def.—2-on-2 screening
5:00 - 5:20	#12—Some Trans. #4 Grant, Inside in Motion
5:20 - 5:25	Game Sit. : DUKE 82 VIS. 77, Vis. 1 F.T., 1:45 left
5:25 - 5:30	Break—Free throws
5:30	8 min. scrimmage
NOTES:	• Training Meal 7:00 • Equipment—Pack Tonight • Thur.: B-Fast—8:30: Leave—9:30

Chapter Four

PLANNING PRACTICE SESSIONS

Seth Greenberg

The first thing, no matter how you do it, is that you must be organized. If you aren't organized, your players are going to know it. There are a lot of different ways to win and a lot of ways to prepare your practice, but if you don't have a method to your madness, your players are going to know it. If you're not organized, then late in the game your players aren't going to be organized. And it's going to cost you. Your method must be consistent with what you are trying to accomplish in practice. There are a lot of different ways to run a practice. I've worked with coaches who have done a bit of everything. One coach never had practice schedules, never told his assistants what was going to be done in practice. He never had anything written, it was all in his mind. But it was very organized. I also worked for a coach who had practices organized to the second. We knew exactly what we were going to do and we would meet for an hour before practice to discuss it. So, you can do it different ways. My biggest thing is that I want my players and my coaches to all be on the same page.

I tell my players, what you do in practice will determine how much you will play. I don't determine that, it's how you practice that determines how much you play. If you want an opportunity to play, then practice well. Practice hard and practice with a purpose. At our first team meeting I tell them that as coaches we do not determine who is going to play. You determine who is going to play by the way you practice. Then automatically they understand that they are the determining factor. I don't believe in stretching. They stretch on their own. They each have their own routine. We have a student manager stretch the team in small groups as they come into the gym. When I blow the whistle, everyone grabs a rope. We jump rope for five minutes. During that time I talk to them. I want to get a feel for how they are that day. I need to know who has problems that day. You must have a feel for your players before the practice begins. We jump for five minutes; one foot, two feet, hops, skips, boxes, etc. I want practice to be fun, but I don't believe that it can be fun unless kids are really working hard. Playing hard is a given. Playing well and practicing well is the goal.

If I'm spending my time in practice motivating and prodding to get my team to play hard, I don't have their ear. We have a sign in our locker room, **"Playing hard is a given. The goal is to play well."** I don't want to spend my time motivating in practice. It's not a debate. Either you practice hard or you lose the privilege to practice and then you lose the privilege to play. I want them to have fun in practice, but the only way that we can have fun in practice is if they are really working. We don't accept anything but that. If you once accept anything but their best, that next day they will find a reason not to play hard. It must come from within. I believe in keeping practice moving. Too many times we stand and talk, and get caught up in our jargon. Make a point and move on. We go from one drill to the next quickly and they know that they must get there quickly. I don't want to waste time. If you need water, get water. If you are not in a drill and you need water, get it. I don't have a five-minute water break. I don't want the players to get stiff. We try to teach the kids how to play first, then we teach them the plays. It's more important for the kids to know the hows and whys and whens. The players need to know the game to be effective.

We have a player notebook that they fill out after practice. We check these books. I treat our players like I expect them to all become coaches. The next thing is the concept that **"almost right is wrong."** Once we teach an idea, we want it done the right way. But how you correct that almost right is going to determine your success. Suppose you teach a concept and then a week later you must reteach it. How you do it will determine your success. If you continually go at them, they will turn you off. How you teach and how you correct will determine your players' attention span. When it is important for you to really bring the hammer down, it's not going to have any impact. So, it's very important that you understand how you are coming across to your players. It's important that they do things the right way, but it is also important that when you correct them, it is done in the right way so they hear what you say. The length of practice is important. For the first two weeks we go for two hours and forty-five minutes. We go three days a week in the morning from 6 to 7:15. In the morning we shoot, do skill work, and teach. It might be the screen and roll or something. It won't be a workout, it will be a teaching session. Then, in the afternoon I don't have to spend time teaching. We can take that concept and drill it. We can keep practice moving. If, in the first two weeks, I spend my time teaching, stop and go, stop and go, the practice never has a flow.

In the second two weeks, we stop going in the morning and we cut back to 2 and 1/2 hours. From December 1st to winter break, we cut to 2 and 1/4 hours. But when winter break comes when they have no classes, we go back to a second practice. That's a time of the year when they don't have classes, study hall, and tutoring sessions, and we have their total attention. We feel we must regroup, make strides and improve. Then, from that time to our first league game, we cut back to two hours. After we've been through the league once, we cut back to 1 and 1/2 hours. I want to keep their legs fresh. We do a lot of teaching and individual work during this time. Included in our practice time is our weight work. We lift two or three times a week all season depending on our game schedule. You tell your players to lift hard in the off season, and they lift hard in the preseason, and then you come to your season and if you don't lift, you lose everything that you built up. So, we include lifting in our practice time. It's very important to me that we lift twelve months a year. We take two weeks off after the season is over and we start again. The stronger they are, the better they are.

If you have a staff, it is important that you all use the same terminology. You must be on the same page. You must get with your staff and discuss exactly how you are going to describe and teach a concept. What is important in your screen and roll for example? You must all be emphasizing the same things. And if you have a junior varsity, and a grade school program, get with your coaches and get on the same page. Terminology is the killer. Things we take for granted, sometimes our players have no idea what we are talking about.

Give each of your assistant coaches an area of authority. For example, I have one coach who watches blockouts. This is the only thing that he is concerned with during a group drill. So each has an area of expertise that carries over into the game. The best thing I ever did with my staff is to have only one person talk to your players about shooting. I don't even talk to my players about shooting. I have one assistant coach who is the only person allowed to talk to the players about shooting.

Everyone teaches it a little differently. So, one coach, and one coach only. Competitive drills, I love competitive drills. If you have one player who is always on the losing team, what does that tell you? He might look the best, and this happened to me. One player on my team this year who looked great never won a drill, ever. But if you just looked at him, you'd say that he has to play. But he never won. And I found out that the other players didn't want to play with him because they knew he never won. If you make drills competitive, you find out who your winners are. You find the people who do whatever it takes to win. And that's important. Conditioning drills. We don't do any conditioning drills without the ball. It's timed, but everything is with a ball. The game is played with a ball. And the players are goofy. If they have a ball, they don't think that they are doing conditioning drills. But, in these drills you have a winner and a loser. How many of you, when you start practice for the year, have a checklist of everything you want to get in for the year? On that list you have when you are going to put them in. You can't just have a checklist, but you must have one when you are going to put them in. You must have a timetable.

You need a progression of drills. There must be a method to your madness. You can't just jump from one drill to another. There must be a logical progression. You must be able to guard the ball before you can contest the lead pass. I like catchy names for the drills, something to identify them. We use something called **"Team and Reminders."** This is the greatest motivator in the world. You wouldn't believe what this does to your practice. If a player takes a charge, dives on the floor, makes an unselfish play, anything that builds the team concept, we give the guy a **team.** You get a **reminder** if there is a loose ball and you don't dive on it, if you make a stupid play, take a bad shot, etc. At the end of practice if you have more **teams** than **reminders** you don't have to run. You can save them, or you can give them to your teammates if they have more **reminders** than teams. If you have two **reminders** you must do a full-court layup, make it, return, make it and do it again in 20 seconds. With some players giving away their **teams,** it is a fun way to develop some team chemistry. We keep track of these for the year and at our end-of-the-year banquet our biggest award was the team award. It's amazing the intensity that this brings to practice.

Twelve Rules for a Successful Practice

- Be positive and good things will happen. That's hard to do every day. A negative thought is a down payment on the obligation to fail.

- Teach every day, the whole season. You must be ready to go the entire season. Don't lose your enthusiasm so the team will improve every day.

- We do defense every day. We do stance work every single day. It doesn't take long, 4 - 5 minutes.

- We block out every single day. We monitor blockout on every drill.

- Be consistent with your personality every day. You can't be their buddy one day and be mean the next. Care about them every day.

- We do skill work every single day. I call it pre-practice. We break out practice into pre-practice, practice, and post-practice. We jump rope and we do pre-practice for 20 to 30 minutes. It's fundamentals; getting open, shot fakes, etc.

- You must have repetition with change. We do some drills almost every day. We will emphasize the same things, but do it in different sets so the kids don't play the play.

- Do drills with a purpose. We stay away from drills for drills' sake. I want drills that are alive, that are reactionary.

- I want carry over from all drills. We do drills that are competitive. After we are done teaching we want repetition, but repetition with change.

- Possession and a half. You must go up and down every day. Run a set offensively, defense converts to offense, and then the offense converts back to defense. If you can get back on defense and take away transition baskets your opportunity to be successful increases dramatically.

- Special Situations - time and score. How many games are won and lost in the last two possessions? If the game is close, who wins? The team who executes at the end of the game.

- Keep it simple. Sometimes less is more. Take two or three things and do them well. We go three days a week with groups of three outside of practice? We spend 30 minutes. We either just shoot or work on skill work. The other thing we try to do, especially over winter break, is to come in in the morning or at 10:00 at night and shoot 100 free throws and have pizza. Make it a fun thing. That's where some bonding takes place.

Chapter Five

THE LITTLE THINGS THAT HELP

Dave Odom

I want to do something a little different from what you normally get at coaches' clinics. I want to share with you some principles of play instead of just X's and O's. The area I think most of us have some difficulties in is the area of **proper spacing vs. pressure defense.** I would like to talk about the principles we follow at Wake Forest. A pressure defense can be half-court, three-quarters court, or full-court. It can be one-on-one pressure like Arkansas plays, wing pressure like Duke and North Carolina, or double-team pressure like Kentucky or North Carolina. I'd like to share things that we use at Wake Forest against these types of pressure.

We follow **six principles:**

PRINCIPLE 1:   Three passes at once.
PRINCIPLE 2:   Attack the double-team.
PRINCIPLE 3:   Numbers on the ball.
PRINCIPLE 4:   Center on the defense.
PRINCIPLE 5:   Block out the defender.
PRINCIPLE 6:   Break the line of the defense.

These principles can be taught in any order. We even warm up with some of these on certain days, depending on who we are about to face.

PRINCIPLE ONE: THREE PASSES AT ONCE

This principle is necessary against double-teams. If you always give yourself three passes, you will be tough to press. In Diagram 1, we set a double-team on the ball at the wing position. The three passes we want are: 1) below and slightly outside the trap; 2) behind and slightly outside the trap; 3) the high post must be on the line of the ball or in the post area if the trap is in the corner. We also have what we call the **Attacker** on the backside, who can attack the basket on the reversal. The player who plays this position must be able to catch, pass, drive, score. We had Rodney Rodgers here this year. This position is important because you'll always be able to get the ball to him in one way or another, and he will have the opportunity to score. A drill we use in teaching our players to handle a trap situation is something we call full-court drill (Diagram 2). We start out with four lines dribbling up and back to loosen up. We allow our players to use any dribble they like. Next, we have them dribble into a double-team at half-court. We place coaches, managers, players at half-court to set the double-team. We tell our dribbler to come to a jump stop, get low, pull the ball into the chest, pivot, and **look through** the double-team. He is to hold this position until the coach blows the whistle. The trap then relaxes and the player dribbles through to the other end. The dribblers then turn and come back, and this time, the trap runs at them, jump, etc.

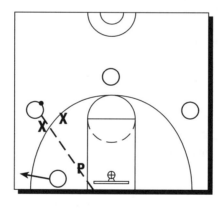

Diagram 1

PRINCIPLE TWO: ATTACKING DOUBLE-TEAMS. We feel there are four types of double-teams we need to be prepared to face. They are:

- North Carolina baseline traps.

- High traps off the pick and roll.

- Double downs.

- Trap ups.

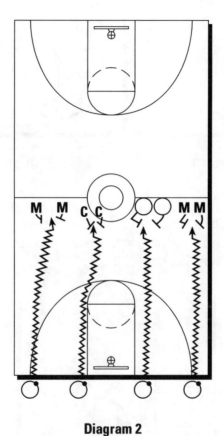

Diagram 2

When facing the North Carolina baseline double-teams, we do the following: the wing drives baseline and the post defender comes over and sets the double-team; we have the offensive post move out and get behind the ball for an outlet off the double-team (Diagram 3).

If the post player is in the low post in this baseline trap, we may move out to get behind the trap or move him up and seal the player who is coming down to help (Diagram 4).

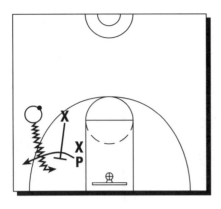
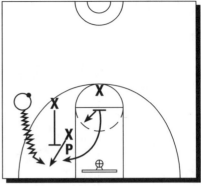

Diagram 3   **Diagram 4**

The post is then to make himself big and look for the ball. If the post is away from the ball when the trap occurs, he is to move toward the baseline and then move up the lane to seal the man coming from the high-to-low-post area (Diagram 5).

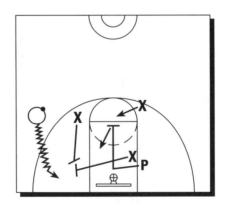

Diagram 5

We will take these three situations and turn them into 2-on-2 or 2-on-3 drills to teach these situations to our players. In dealing with high traps off pick and rolls, we do the following. Anytime you dribble off a high screen, say versus North Carolina, they're going to trap you. We tell our offensive players they have three options:

- **Pick and roll** (Diagram 6) If the screener is not open on the pick and roll, he is to cut to get outside the double-team.

- **Pick and pop** (Diagram 7) After the dribbler comes off the screen and the double-team occurs, the screener is to pop out and look for a return pass. The screener must be a good shooter if you use this option.

- **Step behind the double-team** and reverse the ball to the **Attacker.** (Diagram 8)

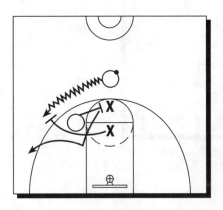

Diagram 6

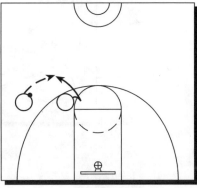

Diagram 7

Diagram 8

- We double down traps; we tell our man who has made the pass that he must get outside and above the trap. The ballside post must move below and slightly outside the trap, and the post on the weakside must line up between the trap and the basket **on the line of the ball** (Diagram 9).

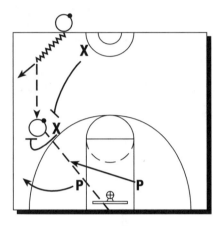

Diagram 9

- Against a **trap up** (Diagram 10). We tell our forward to move out and below the trap; the post must come high on the line of the ball, and the offside wing needs to come all the way over behind and above the trap. When traps come and we get into these options, your continuity is gone and you have to just let your team play. Teams trap you to take you out of your continuity, so if you teach your players how to play, it won't disrupt your game.

PRINCIPLE THREE: NUMBERS ON THE BALL

When I was an assistant at Virginia, and we had Ralph Sampson, we threw the ball to his hand **away from the defense.** We would throw it high so he had to jump to get it. Because he was so light, the defense would push him while in the air so he'd wind up in the corner with the ball. So, we started telling our players to throw Ralph the ball only when they could see both his numbers and he had his numbers on the ball (Diagram 11). We wanted no more throwing away from the defense.

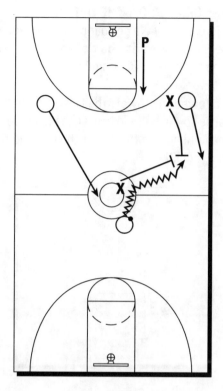

Diagram 10

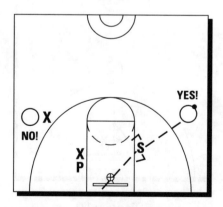

Diagram 11

PRINCIPLE FOUR: CENTER ON THE DEFENSE

Next we want to look at how we get our players **square to the ball.**
We tell post players to **center on the defender.** We want to have the
defender on the line of the ball (Diagram 12).

If the defender is allowed to stay off the line of the ball, he can stop any
move the post makes to the ball. To center the ball, we have the post
cut on the baseline until he's on the line of the ball and then cut up the
line to the ball (Diagram 13).

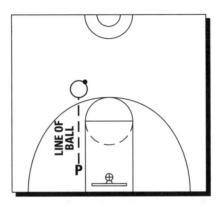

Diagram 12

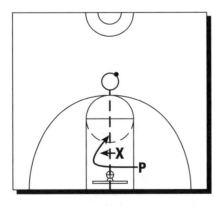

Diagram 13

PRINCIPLE FIVE: BLOCK OUT THE DEFENDER
If the defense is behind the post and if on the pass from the wing, the defender attempts to **run around** the post and get the ball, we tell our players to block out the defender and keep their numbers on the ball if they want the ball.

PRINCIPLE SIX: BREAK THE LINE OF THE DEFENSE
When a guard is double-teamed or the post wants the ball in the lane area, he must come to the ball and get to the **ballside** of the defender. We tell the post he must break the line between two defenders if he wants the ball (Diagram 14). We tell the guard he cannot throw the ball to the post. He (the post) has broken the line between the two defenders.

Diagram 14

A drill we use to teach our players to get on the **line of the ball is:**

3-on-0 full court (Diagram 15).
Here we start with the ball on the endline. 2 and 3 line up on the free-throw line. 2 turns and sets a screen for 3 who comes off 2's screen and breaks to the ball. 3 must be on the line with the ball and 1 passes to 3. After setting the screen for 3, 2 breaks toward the half-court circle and comes back to 3, making sure he's on the line of the ball. 3 passes to 2. 1, after passing to 3, sprints all the way to half-court, makes a cut or

two and comes back toward 2 making sure he is **on the line of the ball.** 2 passes to 1. We continue this all the way downcourt, making sure we don't throw the ball further than 15 feet, making sure we're **on the line of the ball,** and not allowing any dribbling. Make sure to always stress that the receiver is always centered on the line of the ball in order to catch the ball.

We can then turn this drill into a 3-on-1, 3-on-2, or 3-on-3 situation (Diagram 16).

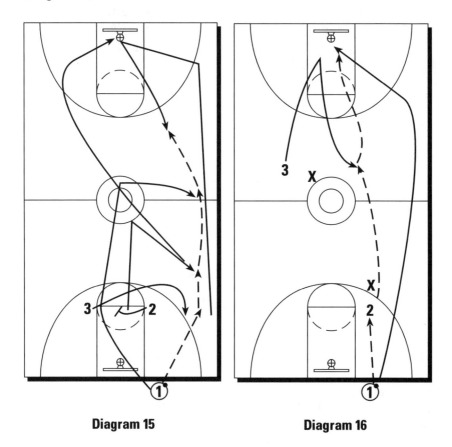

Diagram 15   Diagram 16

Now let's look at good **spacing.** You have the tools for getting the job done, and now you need to be able to apply it (Diagram 17). We have the guards on the outside of the post on one side, and a triangle is set up on the other.

You have good spacing also because you have two on one side and three on the other (Diagram 18). We tell our players that in regard to spacing, **high and wide is better than narrow and deep.** This means that we want to stretch the defense high and to the outside. Why? Because if you take the defense as far as they'll go with you, it will give you room to operate inside. Bad teams have a lot of players around the ball, so if you take them away from the ball, you make it easy to beat them. Against teams that play standard man-to-man defense, that is, one-on-one help-side defense, it is important that you move the defense.

| Diagram 17 | Diagram 18 |

We use a drill called **block offense drill** to prepare for such teams. In this drill, we set up in 1-2-2 set (Diagram 19). We tell our perimeter defense they can do whatever they want. We tell our post defenders they must stay behind the post. This allows us to catch the ball on the block whenever we want. We are working on what to do when the ball is thrown inside.

When the wing passes to the post, he can:

- **Laker cut** (Diagram 20) The wing cuts right at the post and goes either high or low looking for a return pass. If he doesn't get the ball, everyone rotates one position. If you don't want the post to go outside, just have the offside post set a weakside screen for the cutter and stay inside.

- **X cut** (Diagram 21)

- **Double X cut** (Diagram 22)

- **Offset cut** (Diagram 23)

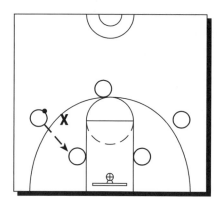

Diagram 19

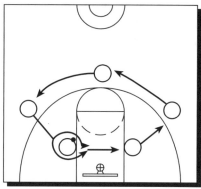

Diagram 20

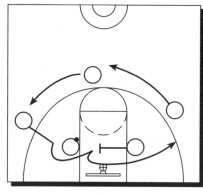

Diagram 21

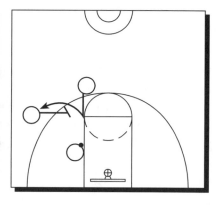

Diagram 22

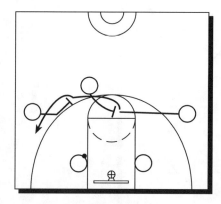

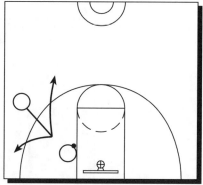

Diagram 23   **Diagram 24**

You use this only with a good shooter at the wing (Diagram 24). The wing must make sure he is always outside the three-point line. This is a good way to teach spacing in basketball. You teach movement on the perimeter and catching the ball inside.

When does the inside player score? He won't have trouble scoring because after you have reversed the ball at least twice, the shots will open up inside. The defense gets lazy and gets out of position. You must teach your players to **be patient** and emphasize to them that teamwork will win out in the end. Let's talk about traps themselves against our 1-2-2 set. As we come across the half-court line, they run a trap-up against us. When this happens, all five players must see this coming and get to our principles. The forward on the point of the ball must step out slightly below and **outside** the trap. The forward away from the ball must come across and be above and slightly outside the trap. The post on the side of the ball comes up on line with the ball and the post away steps out and becomes the **attacker** (Diagram 25).

All five players must see this all at the same time. On a trap down on a pass from the point to the wing, the point must get above and slightly outside the trap. The post on the ballside must step out and be slightly below and **outside** the trap. The post away comes across and lines up on the **line of the ball.** The offside wing assumes the **attacker** position (Diagram 26).

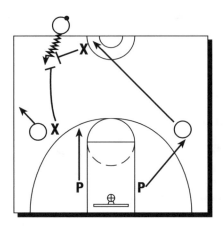

Diagram 25

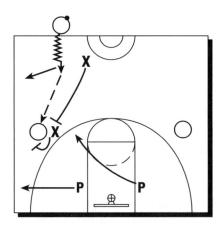

Diagram 26

In attacking the 1-3-1 half-court trap, we set up in a 2-1-2 offensive set. We tell our center that he plays in the middle, and he must take up space and put his back right on the man in the middle to occupy him. Our guard drives up the double-team. The offside guard moves behind and outside the trap. The forward on the side of the ball moves **below** and outside the trap. The center gets **on the line of the ball** and the offside forward is our **attacker** (Diagram 27).

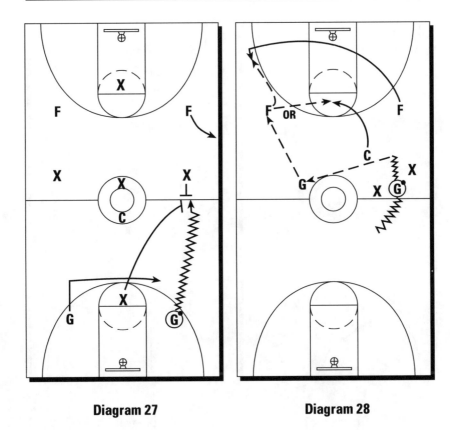

Diagram 27   Diagram 28

In finishing our attack against this pressure, we would **reverse the ball** to the guard behind the trap and have him drive to the opposite sideline. He then looks to pass to the offside forward. The center moves to get **on the line of the ball** and the forward from the opposite side comes across and to the corner, getting **below** and outside (Diagram 28).

The forward may pass to the center or to the forward in the corner. Either would attack the basket. In attacking a 2-2-1 zone press, we would have 5 inbound the ball to 2 and to the center-court circle. 1 would move behind the ball. 3 and 4 have aligned in the corners at half-court (Diagram 29).

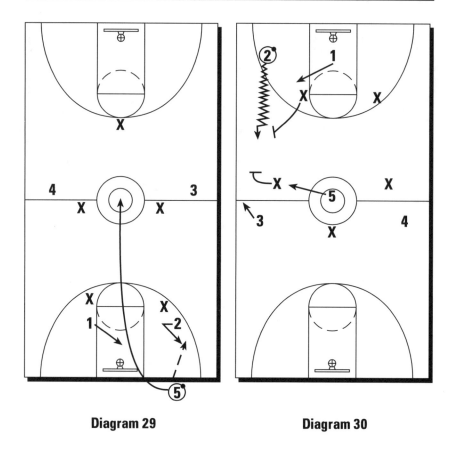

Diagram 29   **Diagram 30**

As 2 dribbles up the sideline and the trap occurs, 1 moves **behind** and slightly **outside the trap.** 3 moves **below** and slightly **outside** and 5 moves **on the line of the ball.** 4 is our **attacker** (Diagram 30).

2 could reverse the ball to 1. 1 dribbles toward the opposite sideline. 5 moves to stay on the line of the ball, and 3 moves to the box on the offside waiting to see where the ball goes (Diagram 31).

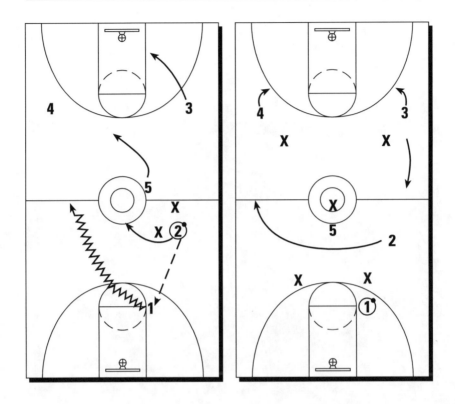

Diagram 31   **Diagram 32**

Our movement is always the same no matter the pressure we confront. Against a 2-1-2 zone press, the only thing we do differently is our alignment. We will convert from the 2-1-2 set we used against 2-2-1 pressure to a 1-3-1 alignment. We do this by having 1 dribble to the middle, 2 swinging to one of the corners at half-court. The forward on the side that 2 moves to drops back and becomes the back line of the 1-3-1 (Diagram 32).

Chapter Six

PRACTICE SESSIONS

Kevin O'Neill

Practice time is when you get your players to really be mentally and physically ready to play. I don't believe you can have a good game team if you don't have a good practice team. I don't believe you can have a good program if you don't have discipline and good things happening in practice. I believe you must convince players that **practice is important.** They must believe that it is the second coming of Bunker Hill. You must spend time year round getting ready for practice. Have a yearly, monthly, weekly, daily plan. We post our practice plans one hour before practice. We do this so that the players can see what's planned, and if they have any questions about the drills, they can ask them before practice. We meet five minutes before practice starts and talk about what is going to happen. We try to discuss three things before every practice: one offensive and two defensive items or two offensive and one defensive item.

To start practice, we always demonstrate one of the things we talked about downstairs in the locker room. The first thing we do as a team is to run two laps and do the **Deep Six** in 31 seconds. This is the only running we do without a ball in practice. Next, we do the following: 2-on-0 full-court passing: chest pass down, bounce pass back, 3-on-0 full-court passing: chest pass down, bounce pass back, 3 and 5 passing: 3 passes down, 5 passes back. If we make any mistakes during these drills, we go back to the Deep Six and start all over.

Next, we might move to what we call the **three-man trapping drill** (Diagram 1). Here we start with an offensive player at one of the corners at mid-court and two defensive players prepared to trap. The coach has the ball at the top of the half-court circle and passes to the offensive player. The two defensive players then move to **trap.** The offensive player must work to get the ball back to the coach. We allow no dribbles, then one dribble, and finally two dribbles in helping the offense get free to pass back. Next, we move to 2-on-0 and 3-on-0 motion drills. We finish up this fundamental segment of our practice with some form of dribbling drills (dribble tag, dribble, etc.).

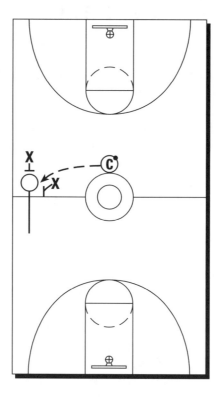

Diagram 1

Four things we cover every day in practice on offense are:

- Movement—passing, cutting, screening.

- Work against a zone.

- Competitive shooting—50 shots (divide team into two groups, first team to 50 baskets wins), two-ball shooting.

- Transition offense—we tell our players that if there are more than two defensive players back, we go into our **secondary break.** If there are two or less back, we run our **primary break.**

We also emphasize four defensive items every day:

- Transition defense—we send three men to the offensive boards and always send our guards back. Teams that play good transition defense will always be in the game.

- Rebounding—3-on-3 competition, 4-on-4 competition, position rebounding. Our administrative assistant only has one job in practice and that is to yell **rebound** every time a shot goes up.

- 5-on-4 **Scramble** (Diagram 2)—five minutes every day.

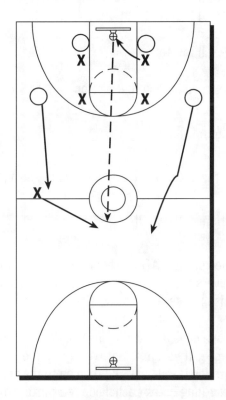

Diagram 2

We have five men on offense and four on defense with another defensive player at half-court. The offense runs our zone offense against the four defensive players. On a made shot, rebound, steal, whatever, the man at half-court takes off. The two guards who were on offense must hustle back to pick this man up. They are not to let him have a layup, or they're in deep trouble. After the first 3-4 weeks of practice, we make this competitive by keeping score. Losers will run. **Situation shell**—4-on-4 shell penetration only. 4-on-4 pass across, screen down 5-on-5 UCLA cut. What we run here depends on the type of offense our next opponent will be running. The four top priorities in our program are: rebounding, defense, good shots, and no turnovers. At the end of practice, we meet at the middle of the floor. We always ask two players to give their evaluation of practice. Players must form two complete sentences in making their evaluation.

Practice rules we follow are:

- No leaving practice without permission.

- No spitting on the ball.

- Always look the coach in the eye when you're being talked to.

- Always run from drill to drill.

- No one-handed passes. After practice we go to our locker room and have two players repeat what we talked about in our pre-practice meeting. This stresses developing attention spans.

After every drill, we have a player sprint to a designated foul line and shoot a one-and-one. If he makes both, we go to the next drill, but if he doesn't, we sprint down and back and then on to the next drill. We give our players a ten-minute break each day in the middle of practice where they must shoot a one-and-one. As soon as they make both, they have what's left of the ten minutes to sit and talk or do whatever they want. At the end of practice, we have competitive team free throws where they are competing for running. When practice is going bad and you want to blow up and just throw them out, which is what they probably want anyway, just stop practice, take them over to the sideline, and sit down and just talk to them about practice, about life, whatever.

Chapter Seven

SOONER INTENSITY DRILLS

Kelvin Sampson

One of the things I always do with practice sessions is to encourage and motivate the kids to play hard. There are certain drills that will do that. Most of our drills are set up with a time element and a goal element. They are not complicated. If anything, I am rather old fashioned in many things that I do.

(Diagram 1) One of the first things that we do is a **lay-up drill.** The only lay-up drills we do are done full-court. This is drawn for the right hand. The rule is that you take four dribbles and lay it up. The next man takes the ball out of the net and goes the other way doing the same thing. I give them five.

This lay-up drill makes them go hard at the beginning of practice. At our summer camps we make the junior high kids go the length of the floor in four dribbles. Obviously they must push the ball out in front of them and go get it. Use two balls going simultaneously. When I blow the whistle, we change direction. So, if someone is going down the floor and the whistle blows, he stops and goes the other way. Now we are shooting the lefthanded lay-up.

(Diagram 2) Two coaches are on the floor. A man takes the ball out of the net, takes one dribble, passes it to the coach, sprints and spots up and receives the pass from the coach. Obviously, if they are not a three-point shooter, you have them spot up closer. Don't promote kids taking **bad shots in drills.**

(Diagram 3) **Two-Man Fast Break**. Pair up your players. Don't ever allow a big person to pair up with another big person. Don't allow

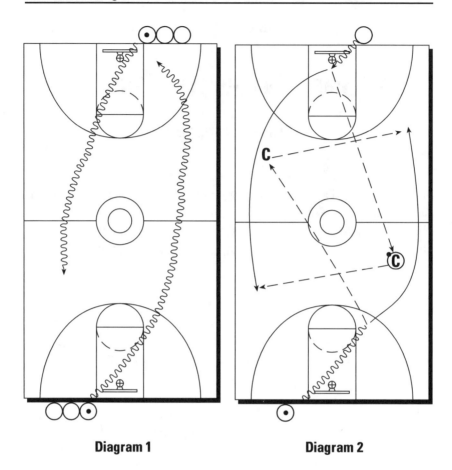

Diagram 1   **Diagram 2**

perimeter players to go with perimeter players. Usually your big players are the lazy ones. They don't think they have to go hard. You need one ball for every two players. 2 makes a two-handed chest pass from the baseline to the elbow. I catches the ball and **looks up court.** Where is the defense? 1 then dribbles to the other elbow as hard as he can. I don't want him taking eight dribbles to get to the elbow. If he can take three and make a **jump stop** and be under control, that's great. 2 sprints down the sideline to the free throw line extended and goes in for the layup. When he shoots the ball, he doesn't stop. He circles to the other elbow and gets the two-handed chest pass from 1, who has become the **rebounder.** They exchange roles on the return back down the court. As soon as one pair gets to half-court the next group goes.

Reverse the drill for the **left hand.** We then do the same drill but we shoot the jump shot or the 3-point shot. Make sure that the pass is made soon enough. The biggest mistake is that the pass is made too late. If a 45-degree **jump shot** is taken, use the backboard.

(Diagram 4) Same drill except that as soon as 1 passes to 2, 1 breaks away to the other elbow and replaces himself, receives the pass from 2 and takes the jump shot. On a 3 on 2 break, it is the top man's responsibility to stop the ball and the back player takes the pass. So, who is open? The passer at the elbow for the return pass from the wing. What do most players do today? They slide down the lane. Now both men are covered. It drives me nuts.

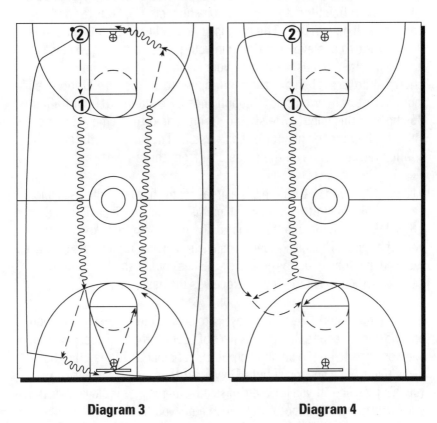

| **Diagram 3** | **Diagram 4** |

(Diagram 5) **Intensity Shooting Drill.** We have a **counter** and a **shooter.** This drill is run for 60 seconds. The counter is not a rebounder. The shooter is his own rebounder. Many of us don't shoot enough.

We forget to let them shoot. The shooter starts out by making a basket. The goal of this drill is to make twelve shots. The shooter takes the ball out of the net, takes two **hard dribbles,** comes to a jump stop. He pivots, shoots and gets his own rebound and repeats. He can go in any direction, but he must go away from the basket. Cover some ground. When he takes the shot he should square up to the basket.

(Diagram 6) **Shooting Drill.** Three people to a basket and two balls. You have a rebounder, a passer, and a shooter. The shooter and passer each have a ball. The goal is to make 14 shots in 60 seconds. If you want to achieve something in your practice, then you must emphasize it. You must motivate your good shooters to become better shooters. The shooter must move from elbow to elbow. He must sprint or he won't get enough shots. He should attempt about 25 shots in this minute. He should sprint, come to a jump stop and shoot. If he reaches his goal, then raise it. They must constantly be challenged. You can run the same drill from three-point range.

(Diagram 7) **Twenty One.** This is a great team shooting drill. Each line has one ball, start at the elbow. Team A is at one end, Team B at the other. We will shoot from four spots. The first team to make 21 shots wins that spot. The losing team runs a sprint. The shooter gets his own rebound and then goes to the end of the line. I want the next shooter to be in a position to shoot when he receives the pass.

I want game speed. I want the players to count. I don't like players who are too cool to count. Counting is part of team unity. It's important that everyone has to do the same thing. You must emphasize that. It's the same thing when you run sprints. Do you let them get away with not touching the line? If you let them miss it by four inches in November they will be missing it by a foot in January. That's your fault. You can't suddenly demand that they touch the line in January.

Diagram 5

Diagram 6

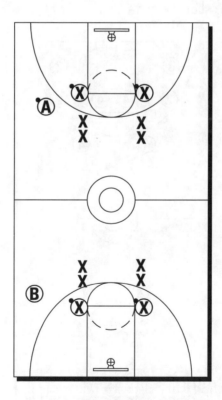

Diagram 7

You must be consistent. That's where some coaches miss the boat. If we don't have discipline in the little things, then we won't have it in the big things. We have coaches to help them count. Sometimes they miss a number. As soon as a team reaches 21, everyone sprints to the next spot.

(Diagram 8) 4 spots. 1 is the elbow. 2 is a 45-degree bank shot. It must be a bank shot or it doesn't count. 3 is near the baseline just inside the three-point line. These are medium-range 15' jump shots. We don't shoot three-pointers from the corner in this drill. 4 is on either side of the top of the key. For the post players, you may need to move them into the elbow. Perimeter people are shooting 3's, post people are shooting elbow jumpers.

Suppose that the score is two to two. The tie breaker is always the 45-degree angle bank shot. You get a lot of shots at game speed in a short

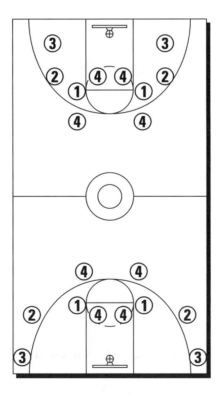

Diagram 8

period of time. We have done all of this in about seven minutes. Look how many shots we have taken at a game pace.

I like to do a shooting drill early in practice, but I also want to do one just before a water break. It is my goal to try get kids to compete a little harder. Try to create an atmosphere where they are going at game pace most of the practice instead of doing things without any purpose. I don't want them just to play hard, I want them to compete.

Give them things to do with a purpose. Give them a goal. If a kid has a goal to make 10 shots and can only make 8, and he must sprint, it's interesting how he always is trying to get to 10. Most players don't know how to play hard and it is your responsibility to teach them. Most likely when this kid makes 10, it's because he put more effort into it.

(Diagram 9) **4-Minute Lay-up Drill.** Our goal is to make 90 layups in four minutes. A, B, C, and D are at the elbows to receive and make the passes. I want a chest pass to start. It not only looks good, but it will probably be a pass that can be caught. This is run simultaneously on both sides of the floor. The players are on a dead sprint. 1 makes the chest pass to A. A receives the pass, pivots and passes the ball out ahead of 1. 1 catches up to the ball and immediately passes to B. B is the most important man. B will give him a drop-step pass, so I can lay it in. We do that for two minutes.

At the two-minute mark we change the passing positions. Make sure that your laziest people don't always get one of the non-running positions. You must pass it cleanly and catch it cleanly to make 90.

(Diagram 10) If we don't get 90 we do the tip drill. We use the heavy ball. Throw the ball against the backboard and sprint to the end of the other line. If we only made 87 lay-ups instead of 90, then we have a three-minute tip drill. This encourages them to go hard in the four-minute lay-up drill. Every drill we run gets them to go hard, to play hard, and to do it together.

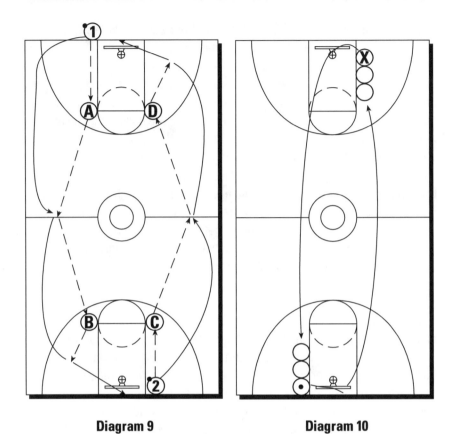

Diagram 9   Diagram 10

Chapter Eight

OFFENSIVE ALIGNMENTS

Wimp Sanderson

Let me mention a few things before I get to the X's and O's.

- Every year, you must lower expectations with the fans and with the press. You'll have to tell your team differently and tell them not to believe what they read in the paper. Don't get yourself in the situation where you tell somebody how good you are going to be. It will get you fired.

- In coaching, X's and O's are important, but coaching is dealing with people. You must be able to work with your kids. They will do just exactly what you let them do. I have two players running at 5a.m. because they skipped class. You must back up what you say you are going to do. That is the discipline part of it. There is only 18 inches difference on the bench between being an assistant coach making suggestions and being a head coach making decisions.

- If you are successful, don't ever think it is because you are the mastermind behind the success of your team. If you are going to win games, I would suggest to you to get yourself some good players. My old high school coach would stand outside the cafeteria and look for players. Get in a situation where you can have a good feeder system to get some players coming into your program.

- Offensive basketball is not an equal opportunity situation. Basketball is equal opportunity for everything except offense. I don't want some players to shoot and some players I want shooting a lot. You must have alignments, know your personnel, and know what you need to do. Some coaches are very successful with the motion offense. I'm not. In the motion offense, I don't know who is going to shoot the ball.

- When you are a head coach, be yourself. Don't try to be somebody else. While I was at Alabama, I saw a lot of football coaches come in and try to be Coach Bryant. All of them got fired.

Here are some things we do with our team. We will work on the skip-pass, improving the passing angle and what we call "check."

(Diagram 1) First of all, I want to skip the ball a lot because of the three-point shot. 1 and 2 both have a ball. 1 passes to 4 in the left corner, moves away and receives the skip-pass back. 4 then cuts to the middle to receive the pass from 1. 4 lays it in. Immediately, 2 will run the same thing to the other side. So we skip it, we skip it back, we cut, we throw it inside and we shoot. We can then change it so that 1 shoots a three-point shot on the return pass.

(Diagram 2) Now we add a post. 1 passes to the baseline to 4 who passes inside to 6. 6 pivots and passes out to the weakside. 6 then cuts across the lane for the return pass from 1. 6 shoots.

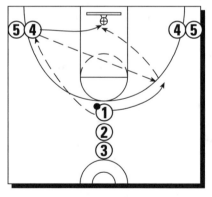

Diagram 1

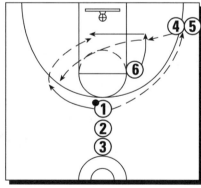

Diagram 2

(Diagram 3) Improving the passing angle with the dribble. The dribble should be used, not abused. 4 is guarded by a manager. The coach will pass to 1 after 1 makes a V-cut. 1 dribbles to improve the passing angle to the post. Surely 4 can seal the manager to get the pass. 4 lays it in. I must dribble with the left hand and make the bounce pass to 4.

(Diagram 4) Same drill except it is run toward the middle. The dribble has taken him someplace, the angle has been improved. These drills really help us to feed the post. In order to get it outside, you must get it inside.

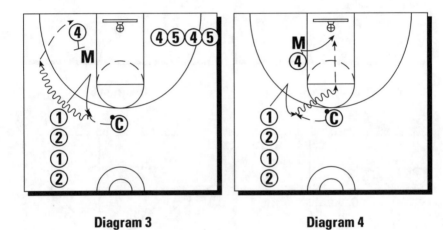

Diagram 3   **Diagram 4**

(Diagram 5) Now the manager is fronting the post. 1 dribbles toward 4 and makes as short a pass as he can. When he makes a lob pass, he throws it to the corner of the goal.

(Diagram 6) We also improve the angle by the use of the pass. 3 passes to 2 and 5 seals his defensive man and receives the pass from 2.

(Diagram 7) If 5 is being defended on the topside, the pass is made from 3 to 4 in the corner. 5 seals his man and receives the pass on the baseline side from 4.

(Diagram 8) Post Pins. Both posts are facing inside. As the ball is entered into center court, both posts have their hands up for the pass. As the ball is passed to the side, the post turns and pins his defensive man and gets the pass from the wing. The next man goes to the other side.

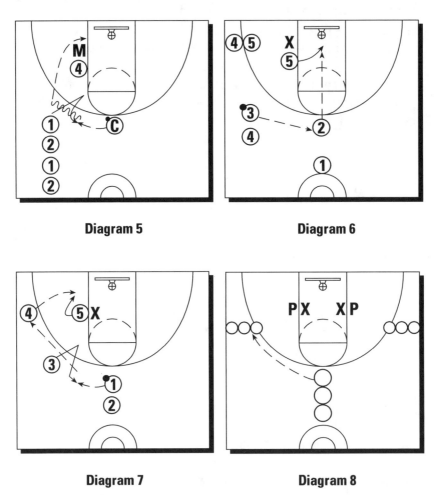

Diagram 5   **Diagram 6**

Diagram 7   **Diagram 8**

(Diagram 9) Now dribble the ball to the wing and pass back with the post working to get open. A variation of this is to have the weakside post flash to the high post.

(Diagram 10) The ball is passed to the wing. If the post isn't open, the post screens away and the opposite post comes high. The other post rolls low.

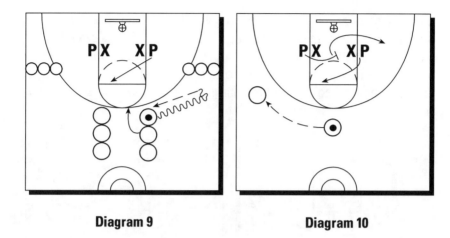

Diagram 9   **Diagram 10**

(Diagram 11) **Checking.** This is where we go to the basket without the ball. 1 is a guard, 2 is a big man. 1 dribbles toward 2 who is overplayed. 2 breaks for the basket and gets a bounce pass from 1.

(Diagram 12) 1 passes to 2 and makes a basket cut. 2 will dribble toward the middle as 1 comes out hard. 1 stops and goes to the basket and gets the bounce pass from 2. Make sure that your kids understand what you want. There are a lot of times that my high school coach would ask me if I understood and I said yes, when I didn't. I wanted him to get on somebody else. Sometimes, we think that the players understand and they don't. I don't know that we allow enough time for shooting today. When Coach Rupp was at Kentucky, they shot for 30 minutes every day, and it was the most difficult period of the day.

(Diagram 13) **Block-out Drill.** The coach will shoot the ball and if the defensive team gets it, they will run a fast break to the other end. Or else you can have the four offensive players weaving the ball outside the three-point line and then one of them can shoot. The defense must block out and get the ball.

(Diagram 14) **Breakdown.** This is 3 out, 2 under. If we got into the middle of an offense and somebody got lost or messed up, we would call out "breakdown" and go into it immediately. I would get into this from a lot of different alignments. I'm showing you this first because this is what I teach the team first. I can pass to either wing, in this case, 1 passes to 2. 1 follows the pass for 2 steps and then sets a downscreen. 4 comes off for a jump shot. 2 could also pass directly to 5. If 4 doesn't have the shot, he looks to 5. If 5's man is pinned behind, 4 passes directly to 5. If 5's man is fronting, 4 can lob to 5.

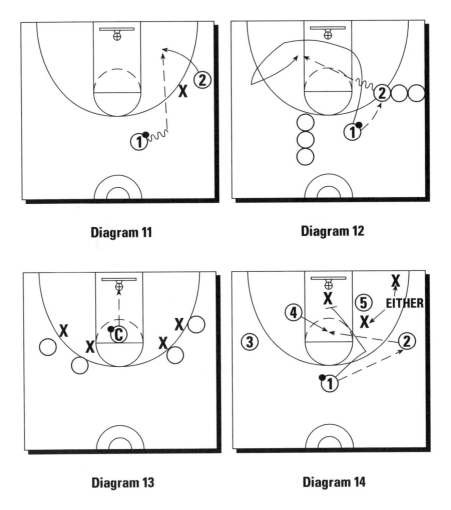

Diagram 11

Diagram 12

Diagram 13

Diagram 14

(Diagram 15) If none of this happens, 4 has the ball near the top of the circle. The more that the ball is in the center of the court, the better your offense is. Do your players know this? 3 down-screens for 1 who breaks out to get the pass from 4.

(Diagram 16) 4 follows the pass two steps and then sets a down-screen for 5 who breaks up into the lane. 1 can pass directly inside to 3 who has posted up, or else pass to 5.

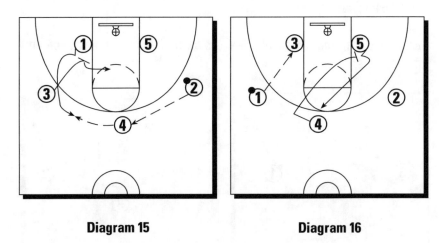

Diagram 15   **Diagram 16**

(Diagram 17) Suppose the defense switches the screen. 2 has passed to 1 and down-screens for 5 who starts to break high. If they switch, 5 cuts low around 4 to the short corner.

Diagram 17

(Diagram 18) If 5 doesn't get it, 5 goes to the wing and 1 will dribble to the top.

(Diagram 19) You can also screen on the ballside. 3 passes and down-screens for 4. 2 improves the angle with one dribble and passes inside to 3.

(Diagram 20) **Pressure release.** 1 dribbles toward the wing who curls around 5 and cuts up the lane.

(Diagram 21) Another pressure release is for both wings to down-screen for the posts.

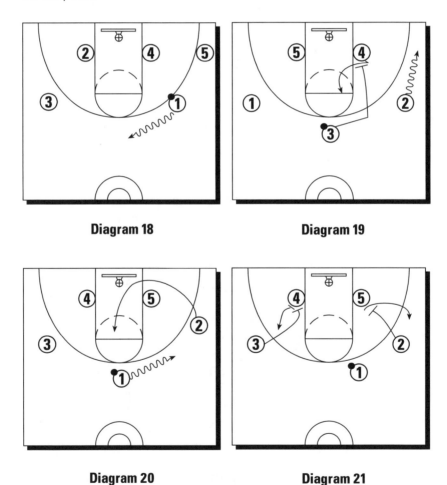

Diagram 18   **Diagram 19**

Diagram 20   **Diagram 21**

(Diagram 22) We can also run this out of the stack. 1 dribbles to the wing. That is the key for this to start. 2 pops up for the jump shot. If 2 does not get the jumper, 2 passes to 3 who breaks to the other wing. 2 then down-screens for 5 who cuts to the ball.

(Diagram 23) 1 can pass to 2 breaking to the wing. 3 then comes off of 4 for the pass from 2. 2 can also make the skip pass to 1 who has flared to the other wing.

Diagram 22   **Diagram 23**

(Diagram 24) I don't like the Flex as an offense, but I like to use a Flex Cut once in awhile. 1 dribbles to the side and 2 curls to the top. 5 sets a screen for 3 who breaks to the corner. 4 flashes to the high post.

(Diagram 25) If no one is open, 1 will pass to 2 who dribbles away. As 3 comes off the screen of 5, 5's defensive man must help. This man is then screened by 4 and 5 breaks toward the ball. One of the best things you can do is to screen the help. 5 should have the jump shot. Don't forget,that when someone is open they can shoot it.

Offensive basketball is getting better shots than your opponent and more of them. Then, you must get to the offensive board. You must get some cheap baskets. Some come off of the fast break, but they also come off the offensive boards. I don't think size is a requisite for being an effective rebounder. I had a player who would get his spot, his opponent's spot and your spot. He would get all three of them. He wasn't a good leaper, but he was a good rebounder.

(Diagram 26) **A Box Set.** 1 dribbled to the wing, 2 will backscreen for 4 who breaks to the low post. 5 clogs the area with a down-screen for 3. 3 will have a jump shot at the free throw line. 2 will move out to the perimeter.

Diagram 24

Diagram 25

Diagram 26

(Diagram 27) Now you are back into "Breakdown." If 3 has the ball, 3 passes to 2 and screens down for 4. You don't have to run "Breakdown." You may want to run from the box to motion.

(Diagram 28) **Pick The Picker.** 5 screens across for 4 and 2 then screens for 5. 1 dribbles to the wing. We are going to backscreen the guy defending 5, or backscreen the player who switches.

(Diagram 29) As soon as that occurs, 1 passes to 2 who dribbles away. 3 comes across and screens for 5. 4 then screens down for 3 who pops up the lane.

Diagram 27

Diagram 28

Diagram 29

(Diagram 30) **Quick hitter.** 2 backscreens, 5 rolls and 1 hits 5. 4 downscreens for 3 who comes to the top.

(Diagram 31) If 5 is not open, 1 reverses to 3 at the top. 3 dribbles as 4 screen across for 5 and 2 then downscreens for 4.

(Diagram 32) **UCLA Cut.** 2 breaks to the wing and 1 makes the pass. 5 sets a screen for 1 who breaks off the screen to the low post. 3 must make a short V-cut before he breaks off of 4's screen. I defend this by not allowing 5 to catch the ball.

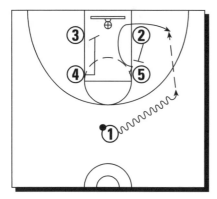

Diagram 30

Diagram 31

Diagram 32

(Diagram 33) You can also run this same play from a "wide" formation.

(Diagram 34) **Shuffle Cut.** I don't think you can have a steady diet of it, but I use it on occasion. 1 passes to 4 who steps out and 1 then cuts off the screen of 5.

(Diagram 35) 5 steps out and 4 passes to 5. 2 screens in for 1 as 4 down-screens for 3. 5 can pass to 1 or to 3.

Diagram 33

Diagram 34

Diagram 35

(Diagram 36) This is almost a shuffle-cut. 5 breaks out and gets pass from 1. 3 comes high and sets a screen for 1. 4 moves across.

(Diagram 37) As soon as 3 sets the screen, 3 pops out and gets the ball from 5. 4 screens for 5 who breaks into the middle. 1 has continued through to the basket and then breaks out to the wing. He can run a "check" at this point and gets the pass from 3 for the lay-up. If not, 3 passes to 1 on the wing or to 5 coming off of the screen set by 4.

Diagram 36

Diagram 37

(Diagram 38) After 4 screens for 5, 4 rolls. After 3 passes to 1, 3 screens down for 4 who has rolled low. We are back to "Breakdown."

When you have a player who can't shoot, you can say "either you are a bad shooter or you are a good shooter taking bad shots." How will he answer? He will say that he is taking bad shots. He won't say he is a bad shooter so you can get him to limit his shooting himself.

Diagram 38

Chapter Nine

ORGANIZATIONAL THOUGHTS

Danny Singleton

Think about these things:

- **No whistles in practice.** Don't use one in practice, you can't use it during a game. Your kids must be attuned to your voice. If you want to stop the play, just say "stop." Don't use the whistle. It means something different on Tuesday night than it does on Monday afternoon.

- **Go to successful coaches practices.** I do this as soon as my team gets beat out of the tournament. I go every day. You need to watch people who win. Don't go watch the coach who is loaded with talent. Watch the coach who is successful without the unusual talent. Watch people who are winning with people like yours.

- **Coach your coaches.** Don't be intimidated by your assistant. I have six assistants and I make them angry every day. They are coaching their kids to prepare their kids to play for me. If we aren't on the same page, we are messed up.

  Get an assistant who is not intimidated by you and who is not afraid to **disagree with you.** I have one who disagrees with me every day. I must have him. He made me change last year, and he was right. I was trying to run some flex and couldn't do it. Get somebody who will cause you to think. You are not that smart. Neither am I. Find someone who will challenge what you are doing.

- **Use teaching aids.** I use everything in the book. I use the Big Ball, dribble glasses, heavy ball, heavy ropes, we've done everything. All good teachers use aids. Use everything at your disposal.

- **Obnoxious parents.** I have two. Know where they sit? On my bench and they are keeping stat charts. That shuts them up. I told one he couldn't come to any more games unless he did what I said. I told him he must sit next to me, keep his mouth closed, and keep a time chart. And he did.

  Don't be afraid to **walk away from practice.** We will be in a drill that is going bad. I won't say a word. I'll just sit for ten minutes. Don't be afraid to be quiet. I'm not afraid to get after my kids, but I'm also not afraid to be quiet.

  During practice, **I never make a substitution.** Before we go on the floor, I put five or six sheets on the wall. I have every person listed for every drill. I don't waste time.

- **Immediate encouragement.** If something happens I don't like, stop and do **"two walls."** We take off. We stop immediately and I encourage them. I also use **explosive jumps.** While they are doing it, I ask them to tell me what playing rule was violated. I changed their behavior immediately.

- **Only one free throw in a row.** No one in America agrees with me on this. We never shoot ten in a row, never shoot two-shot free throws.

What Is Your Philosophy?

In my first coaching job, I didn't know anything. I bought a book called **"Basic Inside/Outside Attacking Offenses."** It had 228 pages. I read the first 43 pages and that's what we did. That was my philosophy, that was my attitude, that's what I knew about basketball. We went 19-5, and I misunderstood the diagrams and had the wrong people in the wrong positions. They had never won more than four games a year at that school. Why did we win? Not because of what we did, but how we did it. I got the kids playing hard, got them loving me, and got them busting it. I got another job at a school and my first year there we went 2-20. After the season, I talked to the old football coach, the most influential coach of my life. He said, "This is how you win basketball games. Every time you get the ball, get a shot." That was his philosophy. That started me thinking. What's important to me? This is what's important to us.

If there is any consolation of love, if there is any fellowship of the Spirit, if any affection and compassion, make my job complete by being of the same mind, maintaining the same love, united in spirit, intent on one purpose. Do nothing from selfishness or empty conceit, but with humility of mind let each of you regard one another as more important than himself; do not merely look out for your own personal interests, but also for the interest of others. Have this attitude in yourselves.

– Paul's writings to the people of Philippi

I am a Christian, I go to church. This doesn't mean that I try to convert my kids. Our attitude is we don't care who scored; we scored. I don't care who got the rebound; we got the rebound. I encourage the kids with their individual stats, but that is our attitude. We want to be unselfish. That's where we start from.

Do your kids keep notebooks? Make the kids keep a notebook and put some things in the book that are important to you at the start. The writing I just gave you is page one, and my kids have to know it. On the first day we circle, and I'll start. I say the first sentence and then point to someone who will give me the second, then I point to another, etc. Here are some things we put in the notebook.

Life's Priorities:
(These are mine)

- Relationship with God.

- Relationship with my wife.

- Relationship with my family.

- Lovett Hoops.

- Private time.

Every kid on my team must fill this in. What happens if one of my kids gets in trouble? He brings in his notebook and we go down the priority list.

Team Hoops Goals:

- State tourney berth.

- 22+ wins.

- Region Champ.

- Sub Region Champ.

- Woodward Westminster Pace.

Individual Hoop Goals:

- Not my plan—our plan.

- Better example.

- Better communicator.

- System more cohesive.

- Sense of pride in my work.

Imagine November 18—What is everyone saying about us after the game? Unbelievably intense and aggressive—fun to watch—fast break hoops—who scored the most points for us? I don't have any idea. Did they get an offensive rebound?

I have the kids write these things. We do things like this every day. What happens is that you get your kids coaching each other in a positive way. This makes a difference. Establish your own personal philosophy and then convince your kids to play the way you want them to play.

Terminology

Is your terminology consistent with what you do? Here's the way we do it. All of our offenses are one digit plus a call. "1 low," "1 high," "1 circle." Our defenses are two digit numbers. Conditions are colors. We use the flag system. We use visual signals as opposed to audible commands because of the noise. We have 19 signals. I give them a test on these. They each have paper and I give them a signal and they write it down. You will be amazed at how many kids won't know them. You know them, but they are not coaches. They are not at a clinic today, are they? You must find a way to teach them what you know. Test them. I'm trying to make you think about what you are doing. Are you an effective communicator? Do your kids know what you know? You aren't going to get them to play if they don't.

Defensive Nomenclature:

All man-to-man is **10 series.**

All zone is **20 series.**

All man-to-man run and jump is **30 series.**

All out-of-bounds situations are **40 series.** We can also go 10 series or 20 series out of bounds. If we say 40-13, it means they full-front with the butt to the ball and with a center fielder, but as soon as the ball is released everybody in the gym yells "ball." If the ball gets in, then we are playing 13 pressure defense. Does your nomenclature allow you to change things on the same play?

10 Man-to-man pressure with help.

11 Man-to-man with one choker.

12 Man-to-man with jump trap and run vs. best perimeter player.

13 Man-to-man full-court/harassment with contain principles.

20 2-3 zone.

21 1-1-2 zone with 1 choker (Y and 1).

22 1-2 zone with 2 chokers (Triangle and 1).

23 2-3 zone with wing trap on one side only/match-up weakside.

24 2-3 zone with jump trap on the point guard and wings.

30 Man-to-man run & jump trap from behind.

31 Man-to-man run & jump trap from behind on the first pass down (G-F entry).

32 Man-to-man run & jump trap from behind when the ball crosses mid-court on dribble.

33 Man-to-man run & jump trap from behind on the entry pass from out-of-bounds.

40 Man-to-man full denial from out-of-bounds with the center fielder (butt to ball).

41 Man-to-man denial from out-of-bounds with the passer being pressured.

Special Calls

Force Finger pointed in direction you force ball.

Choke Hand grasping the throat.

Trap Arms crossed over head.

Hack Hand patting top of head.

OK Universal OK signal.

Out-of-Bounds Plays

This is the only out-of-bounds set we run. The various plays are called by 5. 4 does not call the play.

(Diagram 1) **Power.** 4 takes the ball out-of-bounds. 1, our point guard, is on the back side of the elbow. 2's inside shoulder should be under the edge of the hoop. We lob it to 5. That's all there is. He jumps up, catches it, puts it off the glass. Great shot. We call this a triangle stack. We run this in every situation. 1's move is determined by his defensive man. If his man gets concerned about 5 (1 can see his back number), 1 breaks to the baseline for a short jumper. Something else that happens is that the defense tries so hard to fight through to get to 5 that 2 is open for the layup. It's unbelievable.

(Diagram 2) **Wide.** 2 and 3 go to the corners. 5 goes high. We inbound to the open man. 4 steps under and asks for the power feed from 3 if 3 gets the pass. This is run if 4's defender is sagging off 4.

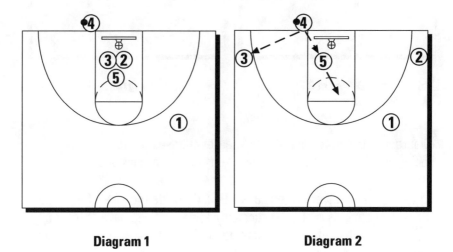

Diagram 1   Diagram 2

(Diagram 3) **High. This complements "Wide."** If 4's defender is playing him tight, 2 and 3 break to the corners. 5 starts out, reverses, and picks 4's defender. If it's a zone, he screens the center of the zone. 4 goes to the high post, 5 seals, and you have a high/low action. That's great against zones. We will shoot the 3 off of this and our opponents know this. So the pass can be made from one of our guards to 4 at the high post and then we get the duck in.

(Diagram 4) **Inside.** What if the center chooses to play in? We back-pick the center with 2 and 5 ducks in off the pick and roll.

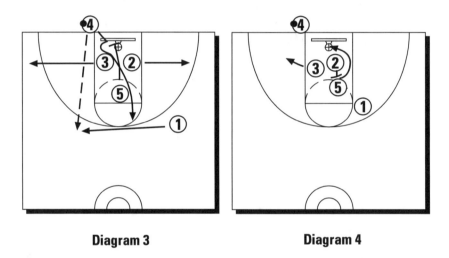

Diagram 3   **Diagram 4**

(Diagram 5) **Outside.** What if the center chooses to play out? We back-pick with 3, 2 influences, and 5 runs off on the pick and roll.

Do you set your players in the out-of-bounds inside the lane? Get close to the basket. This is not a vertical stack, so you don't have to let the defense in. If the defense fights to get in there, back off and read it. Let them in there. We do this night after night after night.

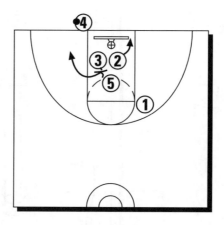

Diagram 5

Jump Ball

(Diagram 6) **Offensive:** 2 and 3 get wide on the offensive end. If you guard both, that means you have two other men left. If you don't doubleteam 4, we are going to tip the ball to 4, who passes to 1 for the offensive break. We never tip the ball forward.

(Diagram 7) **Defensive:** Your player lines up, takes off to the next player on your right. You can steal a tip with this.

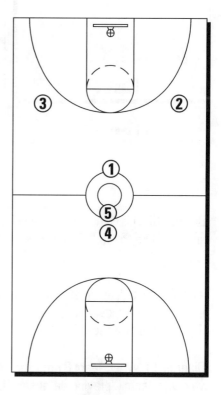

Diagram 6

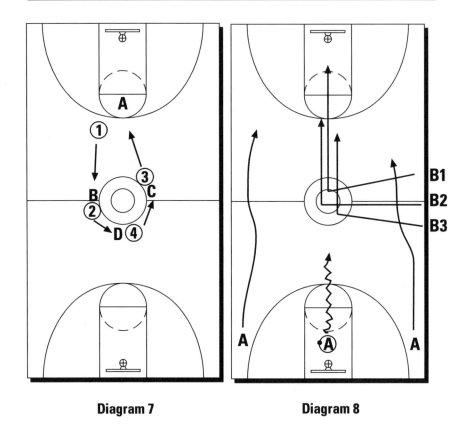

Diagram 7   **Diagram 8**

Drills

(Diagram 8) This is the best transition defense conditioning drill we do. We call this **"The Pride."** The offensive objective is taking advantage of the numbers. The defensive objective is to force the offense to play 3/3.

Team A shoots a layup and runs the break. B1 and B2 run to center circle and retreat in tandem defense. B3 comes into the drill after all three A players have crossed half-court.

(Diagram 9) When Team B gets the ball, they run the break the other way with Team C playing defense. The A Team exits the floor to mi-court and prepares to enter on defense.

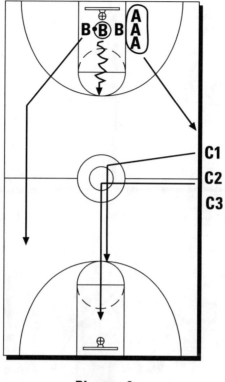

Diagram 9

(Diagram 10) **3-man Shooting Drill.** 2 balls and 3 players. 1 shoots, follows, and passes out to 3.

(Diagram 11) As the ball hits the rim, 2 shoots and follows and passes out to 1. 3 then shoots, follows, and passes out to 2. We do this with a Big Ball, a heavy ball, and a regular ball. This is a contest, 4 goals, 3 to a goal, first team to make a certain number such as 7 out of 10 or 6 in a row. You can do it many ways. Sometimes, I put the guards together and make them only shoot 3-pointers.

(Diagram 12) The **Post Dummy Drill.** The people with the air dummies are beating on the other players. If we can knock him down, we knock him down.

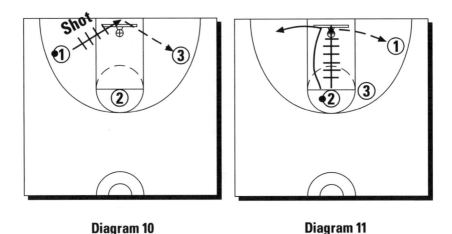

Diagram 10   **Diagram 11**

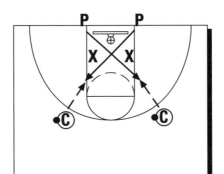

Diagram 12

X = defense w/air dummy.

P = post flash across to low post or high post for entry pass. One side goes low, the other high. Make the move. Score, make outlet pass. Switch lines. If he makes a move to the basket, pound him with the dummy. The ball doesn't touch the floor. Rebound missed shots while being hit with the dummy. Make them hit mid-back to shoulder, never low in the back.

Team Free Throws

12 players on the team, 2/basket, 1 ball. On the command **"team free throws"** they break to the baskets, and by the time I count to 10, the first man must have shot his free throw. They already know who is shooting where. They read the papers posted before practice. In five more seconds, the second man must have shot his. If they miss it, the hand goes up.

(Diagram 13) **Sideline "Gut."** If four or more hands are up, we immediately line up on the sideline. We run the number of "guts" that we miss. There is pressure on the last six players to make that free throw, big-time pressure.

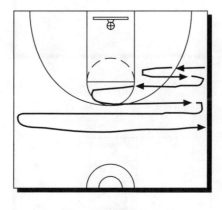

Diagram 13

Offensive Set

5 Set. 5 means 2/3 to us. We have two guards out with three men inside.

(Diagram 14) **5 Double Rover."** 1 and 2 stay from 15' to 18' apart and go wherever they want to outside the 3-point line. 1 and 2 can shoot the 3-pointer. 5 screens for 3. 3 goes wherever he wants to go inside the

3-point line. 4 goes to the **"mesh point"** and tags 3 as he comes off the screen. He literally tags 3. He then goes opposite 3 to the high post, short corner, mid-post, low post, anywhere away from 3. 5 rolls back after the screen. You've got six men in this area, three offensive, three defensive. The defense is going to mis-switch. How many times do you have six players running together? Someone is going to be open.

Diagram 14

Diagram 15

Chapter Ten

PRACTICE PREPARATION

Bob Sundvold

One of the reasons you attend clinics is to refresh yourself on things you know, but could be overlooking. Your season is just over, and a lot is still fresh in your mind. A great thing about our profession is that we continually try to improve ourselves and each other.

We think when we put on a whistle and the coaching shirt the players are automatically going to listen to us. Why should you be heard by your players? I was at a USA Coaches Clinic several years ago when Debbie Holley spoke on this topic. Think about it. In college, I've recruited my players, so I naturally assume I have sold them that maybe I can coach and the school is a good place to be. But, they may not be sure and you must sell them. The first thing I ask myself is, **"Do I care?"** Do I care about the person? Not the player, the person.

Are the things I am doing in the best interest of that person? How do you expect someone to listen to your game plan when they don't take your advice about going to class and being on time?

Players of the nineties are growing up on TV and computer games. You don't have **competition** anymore. There is a **reset button.** If a kid is disappointed with how he's doing, the easy way is to reset and start over. They are more attuned to what's going on with the video game and on TV and competition is nowhere to be found. You must be prepared for this. You must **create competition.**

The players will be satisfied with whatever you **tolerate.** If you let them play **sloppy,** they will. If you let them take **bad shots,** they will. If you don't let them do it, your players will do that, too. If you don't tolerate mistakes, your players will be happy to do that because they really want to win.

What you are doing now is the **key.** You are starting an overview for next season, a master plan. Decide now what you want to do next year. Make a master plan for the year and go through everything from stance to drills.

Once we get into the season, I record what days I did the drills. For example, the 4-man shell drill. I have listed floor position, off the ball, ballside, inside cut, screen away, vertical or horizontal screen, help and recover on the dribble, baseline drive, post defense, etc.

You have a new team in your conference, a new coach moving in. Where's he from? What did he do at his last job? Do you have anyone who stands out that must be covered early? Practices are for coaches; games are for players. You may be thinking about a game in late March and are preparing for it in November. Players are thinking about finishing practice. Prepare to add a play or two in February, maybe add a defense. You can't do the same thing in February that you do in November.

Think about utilization of staff and facilities. How can you **maximize** teaching and learning and **minimize** the time? Our maximum practice time is two hours and fifteen minutes. How many managers will I have? How many assistant coaches will I have? How many volunteers will I have?

Thirty minutes prior to the start of your practice is the most important time for you as a coach in setting your frame of mind for how you are going to teach. Do you want to just **"get through"** a practice? Don't have an early morning 8:00 a.m. Saturday practice. Your players aren't going to go to bed early to get ready for that practice. By the time practice is over, you'll be mad.

Set up a practice so it is the best two hours of that player's day and the best two hours of your day. I write up the practices the night before, often immediately after practice. I share this with my staff the next day. I get feedback from them so when we go on the floor, we have a definite plan. Our drills are short. Individual drills are four to five minutes and a team drill is 10 to 12 minutes. We use **transition** in our drills. If you are working on rebounding, take it to the other end. By mid-season, it drops to an hour and a half and at the end of the year, we drop to 45 minutes. Keep the players fresh and enthused.

This is my version:

Practice #:	Day:	Date:

Emphasis of the Day:

Thought for the Day:

Stations

A:

B:

C:

D:

Time	Subjects
2:15 p.m.	Defense
3:15 p.m.	Offense
4:15 p.m.	Whatever...

Stations refer to pre-practice time. The **emphasis** of the day could be **getting back** on defense or **contesting** shots. Our pre-practice changes. For example, we could have **form** shooting. How many times do your players get to come on the floor and shoot twenty 6' shots, just like you teach in summer camp? A station could be **rope jumping.** Another could be six trips up and down the floor dribbling for a **layup, crossover moves,** etc. A station could be working on **stepping through** a doubleteam, working against a **trap.**

We take a day off during the middle of the week and practice on Sunday. We have a lot of out-of-state kids, and they don't have much to do on weekends when the in-state players go home. If a player isn't on time and doesn't get finished with stations, he remains after practice to finish. We seldom have a post practice for an individual. Players look at it as punishment. If we keep someone, it is only for offense, usually **shooting.** We always stay if a player asks for help.

Chapter Eleven

The Daily Practice Schedule

John Wooden

Part One: Defense

Where there is jealousy and selfishness, there is disorder and evil, and where there is lack of discipline and respect for authority, there will be disorder all the time.

3:00 - 3:29 Individual Attention. Guards and Center work on defending in on the post (Splitting the Post). X1 uses his left hand to protect against a direct pass into the post. X2 drops off and has his right hand placed to protect against bounce pass. (Diagram 1)

Diagram 1

When the guards split the post, the defensive guards make an automatic switch (Diagram 2) with X1 picking up 2 and X2 picking up 1.

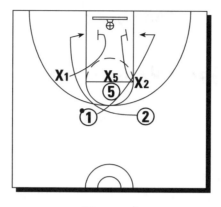

Diagram 2

If one guard splits and the other breaks out, you would defend by X1 keeping his man and X2 coming over the top of the screen to stay with 2 (Diagram 3).

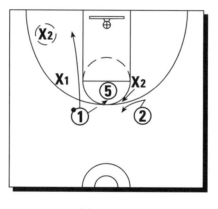

Diagram 3

If 1 and 2 both fake split and then break wide, X1 and X2 must stay with their man. (Diagram 4)

Forwards are working to get open on the **Side Post** and the defense is working to get open on the Side Post while the defense is working on defending the side post. If the forward is being played tight, he can reverse (Diagram 5).

Diagram 4

Diagram 5

3:29 - 3:30 Fundamentals. Coach blows the whistle and players rush to line positions.

3:30 - 3:50 Fundamentals (Diagram 6)

1. Stretching.

2. Imaginary jump shots.

3. Imaginary rebounding.

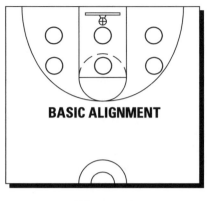

Diagram 6

4. Push-ups (5 times).

5. Change of pace/direction (Diagram 7).

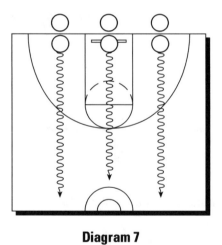

Diagram 7

6. Jump stops (Diagram 8).

7. One-on-one (Diagram 9).

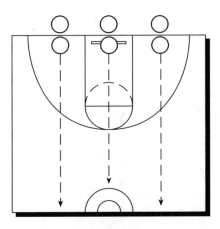

Diagram 8

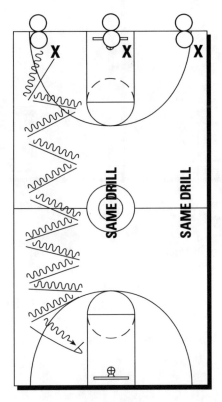

Diagram 9

8. Dribble with the head fake up first, 2 or 3 dribbles, jump stop and then go again (Diagram 10). Next group be ready to follow.

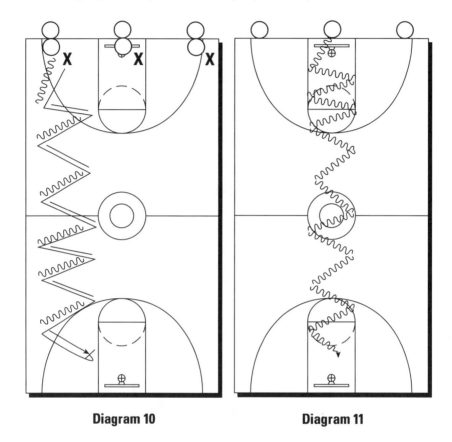

Diagram 10   **Diagram 11**

9. Dribble with hesitation and go, switch hands on dribble (Diagram 11).

10. 4-on-4 break with the trailer-shooting a jump shot (Diagram 12). Coach shoots the ball and 3 gets the rebound. 3 passes to 1 who cuts away and breaks back to the ball. 1 passes to 2 as 1 and 4 fill the outside lanes. 2 drives the ball down the middle as 3 trails. 3 calls right or left, whichever way he is going to go, and 2 passes to him for jump shot.

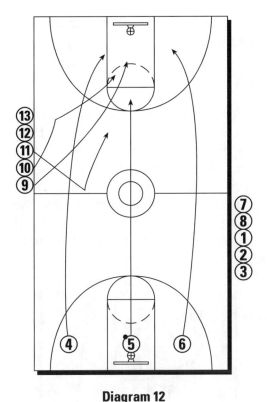

Diagram 12

3:50 - 4:00 Defend the Passing Game

Some of the players who are not in the top 7 or 8 have been working on the **passing game,** as some of the teams will use it against us. We will now put them in to use the passing game as we have the top 7 or 8 who are going to do most of the playing for us until the games are won or lost. That is my **philosophy** again. I tell my players this when I recruit them, and then about two weeks prior to practice, I tell them again. If they can't accept that, they shouldn't be out here. Be patient in selecting who these top 7 or 8 may be. Don't make up your mind too quickly, but once you have made up your mind, be patient with them. **Don't take them out on their first mistake.** If you took two weeks, five weeks or whatever to decide who you were going to play, then take that long before you decide that you were wrong. Give them a chance! Work 5-on-5 against the passing game and work on weaknesses that show up in defending it.

4:00 - 4:10 3-on-2 Conditioner Drill

(Diagram 13). 1 starts the play by rebounding the ball off the board and driving the ball quickly downcourt. As 1 rebounds the ball, 4 moves out and takes a deep spot near the basket and 5 takes a spot in the outer half of the foul circle. When all three offensive men have passed the center line, 6 comes in from the sideline and touches one foot in the center circle and then comes back to help defensively. This forces the three offensive men to attack the two defensive men quickly and get a good shot before the extra defensive man gets there to make it three-on-three.

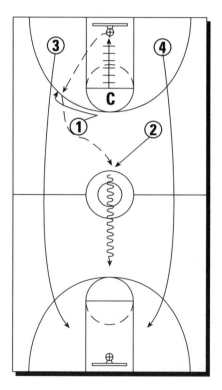

Diagram 13

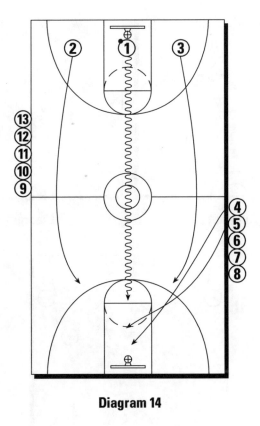

Diagram 14

4:10 - 4:20 Shooting - Special Shooting Drill

Divide the team into three groups. They will shoot the following shots. 1) Baseline (Flat shot), 2) Off the Board, 3) Semi-Circle. They will all shoot the same type of shot at each of the three baskets. The first group to make 15 is the winner. The first two in each line have a ball. The shooter rebounds his shot, passes to the next man in line without a ball and then moves to the opposite side. They rotate to a different basket after each game (Diagrams 15, 16, 17).

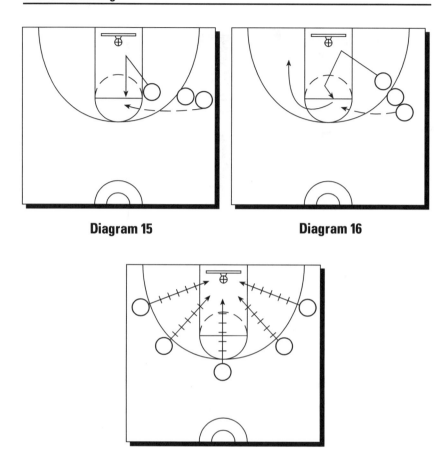

Diagram 15   **Diagram 16**

Diagram 17

4:20 - 4:30 Strongside Defense with the "Out Guard"

Working on defense against the High Post Offense. You would be doing the same thing that you normally do on offense, but today the concentration is defense, whereas the day before it was on offense.

4:30 - 4:40 Work on the Press

Earlier I broke down the **parts of the press.** Let's say we are in the 2-2-1 press. They will be in this position (Diagram 18). This is just our normal press and positions we will be in, but we will start by being in the **High-Post Offense** and stress a particular segment of the offense. We will run that phase of the offense, and when we score, we will just work on getting to the predesigned pressing position in our 2-2-1 press. (Diagram 19). When the offense scores, a coach throws the ball in quickly to emphasize the importance of the players quickly getting to their pressing positions. Say the ball comes in to a guard, X1 and X2 come in on the ball and X3, X4 and X5 drop back to cover.

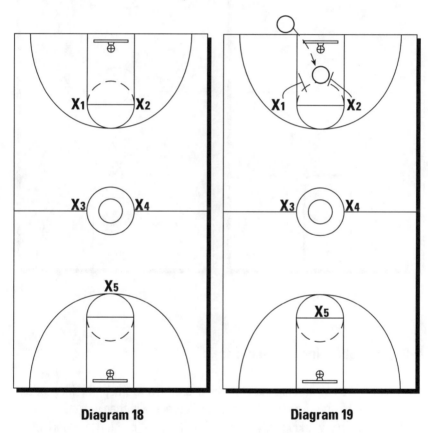

Diagram 18   **Diagram 19**

(Diagram 21) When we call "trap" we now cut off the outlet pass with 1 and 2 playing for a steal (Diagram 20). We may call **"single trap,"** which is nothing more than a 1-2-1-1 trap. (Diagram 21). We want to build in them a feeling of false security against our press and not be ready when we make a change (i.e., 1-2-1-1). Once the ball comes in, all presses are basically the same. X5 calls the defense; he is the "director."

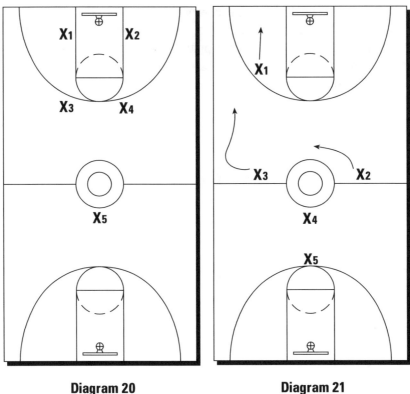

Diagram 20   **Diagram 21**

4:40 - 4:45 Shooting by Positions

The team will break into groups with the guards in one group, the forwards in another and the centers in still another. Each group will then work at separate baskets, working only on the shots they get in the framework of the offense. 3-on-3 from the end line. No long passes are allowed and very little dribbling. This drill teaches footwork, balance and keeping your head up. A lot of these drills have more to them than they seem. When they get across the center line, they switch from offense to defense and come back with offense, now defense, now offense, etc. (Diagram 22)

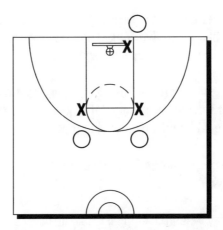

Diagram 22

4:45 - 5:00 Team Fast Break vs. the 1-1-1 Defense
(Diagram 23)

The offensive men will be set in the **High-Post Offense** and one of the coaches will take a shot. The rebounder will look for an outlet pass as the one defensive man is there to challenge until the ball gets to the top of the key. Now the middle defensive man is there and finally the third defensive man picks up the break once the offense gets into the scoring area. This can also be done with a 2-1-2 defense.

Diagram 23

5:00 - 5:15 Defense Stanford's passing attack and fast break when you get possession of the ball. Earlier we worked on defending the passing game and now we are defending the passing game and breaking.

5:15 - 5:25 Defense California's 1-on-1 attack and fast break when you get possession of the ball. We know Cal is going to do a little more 1-on-1 movement so we will work on defending that.

5:25 - 5:30 Each player makes five consecutive free throws and then gets into the shower.

This has been a day when the emphasis for the most part has been on **defense.** On a defensive day, the emphasis on defense comes mostly in the last half of the practice when we are working 5-on-5.

Part Two: Offense

Things that are important in regard to practice.

a.   Be dressed, on the floor and ready for practice on time every day. There is no substitute for industriousness and enthusiasm.

b.   Warm up and then work on your weaknesses and shoot some free throws, then you take the floor until organized practice begins.

c.   Work hard to improve yourself without having to be forced. Be serious. Have fun without clowning. You develop only by doing your best.

d.   No cliques, no complaining, no criticizing, no jealousy, no egotism, no envy, no alibis. Earn the respect of all.

e.   Never leave the floor without permission.

f.   When a coach blows the whistle, give him your undivided attention and respond immediately without being disconcerting in any manner.

g.   Move quickly to get into position to start a new drill.

h.   Keep a neat practice appearance with shirttails in, socks pulled up, hair cut short, clean shaven and fingernails short.

i.   Take excellent care of your equipment and keep your locker room neat and orderly.

j.   Do things the way you have been told and do not have to be told every day. Correct habits are formed only through continued repetition of the perfect model.

k.   Be clever, not fancy. Good, clever play brings praise while fancy play brings ridicule and criticism. When group activity is stopped to correct one individual, pay close attention in order that you will not require the same correction.

l.   Condition comes from hard work during practice and proper mental and moral conduct.

m.   Poise, confidence and self-control come from being prepared.

Practice Planning

a.   Start the practice by warming up.

b.   Close the practice with team drills.

c.   Vary the drills every day so they don't become monotonous.

d.   Explain the purpose of the drills and you will get a better response.

e.   Don't continue the same drill too long.

f.   Teach in small doses and give these doses frequently.

g.   Follow difficult drills with easier drills and vice versa.

h. Teach new things early in practice when players are still fresh mentally and physically.

i. Stress shooting drills every day.

j. Stress fundamental drills daily.

k. Analyze each day's practice while it is still fresh in your mind (before you leave, work out that day).

l. Early season practices are progressive in intensity and build up as you get nearer to playing games.

m. Use small organized groups of 3 to 5 players in teaching the fundamentals.

n. Don't have 4 or 5 players standing around while 6 are working; have them all working all the time.

o. Shooting drills should be game-like (and working in pairs rather than alone).

p. Stress defense and offense on alternate days, but still work on each daily.

q. I believe, and have said many times, that most of our championships were won on defense.

r. How many of you coaches spend more time on defense than on offense? Offense takes more time because you must do things with the basketball. You have to learn to shoot the basketball, pass the basketball, dribble the basketball, protect the basketball, stop and turn with the basketball. You don't have to do these things on defense. There is no question in my mind that the coach who spends more time on defense is not using his time properly. They are equally important, but it takes more time for offense than it does for defense. This is because of the object involved (the basketball).

s.   On days when offense is emphasized, the top 7 or 8 players will be on defense and second-line players will work offense. Many things I have mentioned here apply to both offense and defense.

t.   When players come on the floor, they have been told certain things they need to work on. Early in the year, they shoot a number of free throws in succession to develop a rhythm and style for each individual - later on they seldom shoot many in succession, usually 1-on-1 or sometimes 5 or 10 in succession.

I selected a practice and went back to a practice in my last year of coaching. Some of you might be familiar with some of the individuals I had that year. This day was a Tuesday, January 14, 1975.

3:00 - 3:29 Individual Attention and Free Throws
(Diagram 24)

W -Washington   C - Coach   D - Drollinger

Drollinger and Washington work on deep post moves from both sides (10 shots each side) after receiving pass. Washington - Option 1. He goes opposite pressure for lay-up, hook or power shot. Option 2, after receiving the pass, Washington feels no pressure, so he faces up and shoots bank shot.

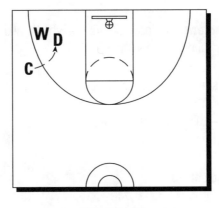

Diagram 24

Also working at this time are McCarter and Trgovich on pulling up at the top of the circle under control (Diagram 25).

T- Trgovich   Mc - McCarter

Each has a basket and drives hard to the basket, stops under control and then shoots a jump shot on balance. (Shoot about 20 in this manner.)

This day the special attention is with the guards and centers; the next day it would be with the forwards. It will vary from day to day with different individuals.

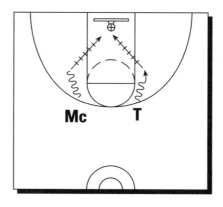

Diagram 25

3:29 - 3:30 Fundamentals. Coach blows the whistle and the players rush to line positions for fundamentals (Diagram 26).

3:30 - 3:35 Stress **proper execution** of each of these fundamentals.

1. Loosening up—stretching all the muscles in
    the body.

2. Imaginary jump shots.

3. Imaginary jump shots off the drive.

4. Imaginary rebounding.

5. Imaginary rebounding with release pass.

6. Imaginary jump ball.

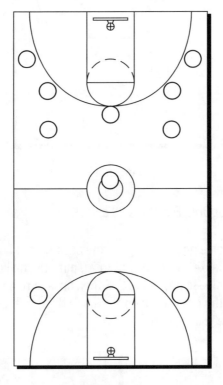

Diagram 26

3:35 - 3:40 Ante-Over Drill (Diagram 27). 1 tosses the ball high above the basket and across and off the board to the basket across and off the board to the opposite side, then moves over to the end of the 2 line. 2 times himself to rebound the ball at the height of his jump and flicks across high off the board to 3 who has moved up to take the place of 1. Keep tipping with each rebounder going quickly to the end of the opposite line as soon as he rebounds. When 30 rebounds are completed, they all move to the free throw line and shoot one free throw each and back to ante-over drill except now it is one-handed (righthanded on the right side and lefthanded on the left side).

Diagram 27

Rebound-Pass Out Drill (Diagrams 28 and 29)

Fake away and come back looking for the pass from 1. 1 then fakes away and goes to the basket for a pass from 2. 1 puts the ball on the board and rebounds it and release passes to 2. 2 then passes to 4 who fakes away before receiving the pass. Then do the same thing to the opposite side. Rotate to the line you pass to.

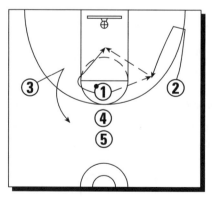
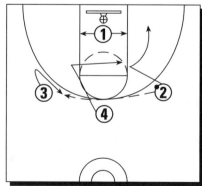

Diagram 28   **Diagram 29**

3:40 - 3:50 Front and Side Drill

Option 1 (Diagram 30). Start with 1 throwing the ball on the backboard and making the release pass. 1 passes to 2 who has made his cut. 2 passes to 3 who faked down the floor and then comes back to meet the ball. 3 then passes to 1 who drives the ball down the middle with 2 and 3 filling the lanes. 2 and 3 should not be even so 1 can look for the lead man and if he isn't open, then look for the other man. The side man should take an 18' board shot.

Option 2 (Diagram 31). Same as option 1 except this time 3 fakes the pass to 1 and hands off to 2 who drives it down the middle. 1 and 3 then fill the lanes.

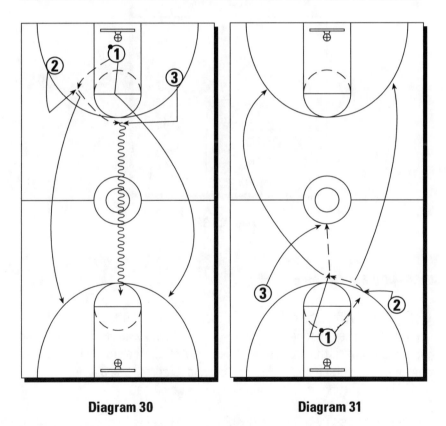

Diagram 30   **Diagram 31**

Option 3 (Diagram 32) This time 3 looks for 1 and 2, but neither is open, so he drives it down the middle himself.

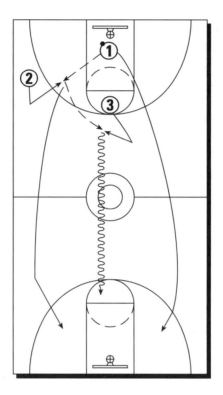

Diagram 32

3:50-4:00 Set Offense

Back-Door (When the other guard is being played tight). 3 flashes to the top of the key to receive the pass from 2. 1 who was being played tight goes hard to the basket as 2 passes to 3 who then looks for 1 on a backdoor. If 1 isn't open 3 looks for 2 cutting (Diagram 33). 3 is now looking for 1 cutting off the doublescreen set by 4 and 5.

If 1 isn't open, 5 sets a screen for 4 and 3 either passes to 4 coming off the screen or 5 on the roll (Diagram 34).

Diagram 33   **Diagram 34**

Forward-Guard Screen and Roll (The forward initiates it by coming up and screening for the guard). 4 comes up to screen and roll as 2 receives the pass from 1. 2 has the option of shooting or driving off the screen or passing to 4 rolling to the basket (Diagram 35).

If he isn't open for the shot or pass to 4, 2 passes to 1 who passes to 4 coming around the doublescreen set by 5 and 3 (Diagram 36).

Diagram 35   **Diagram 36**

Forward Reverse (The key-guard dribbles hard toward the forward being overplayed.) 3 fakes to meet the ball and pushes quickly off his outside foot. He moves quickly for the basket, turning toward the inside so that he never loses sight of the ball when 1 starts to dribble toward him. 1 passes to 3 immediately if he is open. If he isn't open immediately for a pass, 3 **"buttonhooks"** at the foul lane and looks for the pass (Diagram 37).

If 3 doesn't get the ball on the **"buttonhook,"** he crosses the foul lane and comes around a doublescreen set by 5 and 4 and looks for a pass from 2, to whom 1 passed. (Diagram 38)

Diagram 37

Diagram 38

Diagram 39

Zone Attack (1-3-1) also used in Man-to-Man Attack. This play is initiated when 2 passes to 1 who passes to 4 on the High Post. When 4 receives the ball, 5, 3, 1 and 2 all move to the seams. 4 looks for 5 on the deep post first, next for 3 in the seam and thirdly, for 1 and 2 in the seams (Diagram 39).

4:00 - 4:05 3-on-3 Front-Line Guard Break

X1 takes the rebound and passes to 1 who has made his cut. 1 passes to 2 who has faked down the floor and then comes back to meet the ball. 2 drives the ball hard up the middle with 1 and X3 filling the outside lanes. Three players are at the opposite end to play defense against the break (Diagram 40).

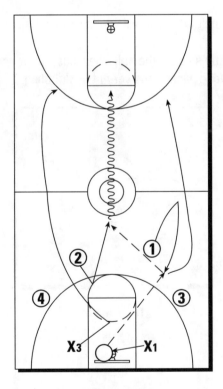

Diagram 40

4:05 - 4:15 Shooting Drills by Positions

The team will break into groups with the guards in one group, the forwards in another and the centers in still another. Each group will then work at separate baskets, working only on the shots they get in the framework of the offense.

4:15 - 4:25 3-on-3 from Center (Diagram 41)

Rules on Defense:

1. Don't allow anyone to dribble **between** you.

2. Don't let them dribble **around** you (outside men).

3. When the defense gets the ball, they must get it across the center line with no long passes and very little dribbling.

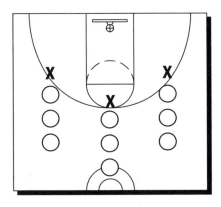

Diagram 41

4:25 - 4:35 3-on-3 Strongside Defense (used every day in High-Post Offense) (Diagram 42)

Rules:

1. Guards may **feed** the post, then may screen for each other, etc.

2. Offside guard is an **outlet** man only.

3. **Rotate** from offense to defense.

4. Go from defense to the **end** of the line.

5. Work both sides of the court, but only use **one side** of the court at a time.

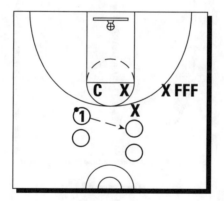

Diagram 42

4:35 - 4:45 3-on-2 Conditioner Drill

They line up as indicated in Diagram 43. 1 starts the play by quickly rebounding the ball off the board and driving the ball quickly downcourt. As 1 rebounds the ball, 4 moves out and takes a deep spot near the basket. 5 takes a deep spot near the basket. When all three offensive men have passed to the center line, 6 comes in from the sideline and touches one foot in the center circle and then comes back to help defensively. This forces the three offensive men to attack the two defensive men quickly and get a good shot before the extra defensive man gets there to make it three-on-three.

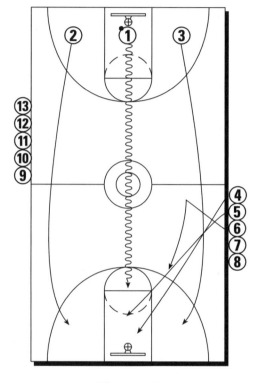

Diagram 43

When the offense scores or loses the ball in any manner, they get off the floor and go to the end of the line at the side. The three defensive men, 4, 5 and 6, now become offensive men and break for the other end as 9 and 10 move out on defense at the other end and 11 becomes the late defensive man (Diagram 44).

4:45 - 5:00 Pair up for **quick jump shots,** two or three pairs at each basket. They retrieve their own shots and shoot two quick shots underneath. Also done with jump shooters using a head fake before the shot.

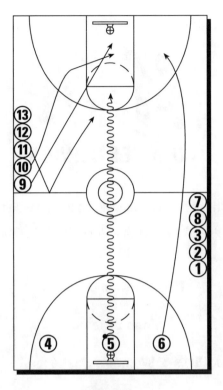

Diagram 44

5:00 - 5:10 5-on-5. Offense will work against a 1-2-2 and 2-3 zone. Each time the offense scores, they will quickly set in the press.

5:10 - 5:25 5-on-5. Offense will work against a Man-to-Man defense. Offense presses after each score.

5:25 - 5:30 End the practice on an happy note by running the full-court five-man fast break with a jump shot. When they execute the break correctly twice in succession with each player being in his assigned spots and the jump shot is hit, the workout is completed.

COACHES CLINICS

If you enjoyed this Practice Planning book, you won't want to miss these other great titles from the USA Coaches basketball library:

Man-to-Man Defense

Zone Defense

Girl's & Women's Basketball

Match-Up Defense

Zone Offense

Developing the Fast Break

Special Situations

Pressure Defense: Volumes 1 & 2

Additonal information on other products in the USA Coaches library, including books, videos and CD-ROMs, can be obtained by either calling 1-800-COACH-13 or faxing 1-314-991-1929.